Here's what people are saying about Barbara Valentin's *Assignment: Romance* books:

"*False Start* was such a wonderful romantic comedy and even though there isn't an ounce of steam in it. I completely loved it! 5 stars!"
—*Boundless Book reviews*

"I had a hard time putting (*Help Wanted*) down. That's probably why I had no trouble reading it in two days! I'll also stubbornly admit that I got a little teary-eyed towards the end, and I absolutely loved the ending. It was the perfect finish and one of my favorite endings, hands down."
—*Chick Lit Central*

"Barbara Valentin delivers love, laughter, and a happily ever after—what more could you ask for?"
—Gemma Halliday, *New York Times* bestselling author

BOOKS BY BARBARA VALENTIN

Assignment: Romance books:

False Start

Help Wanted

The Plate Spinner Chronicles
(a collection of "Plate Spinner" newspaper columns)

THE PLATE SPINNER CHRONICLES

A Working Mother's Epic Adventure

BARBARA VALENTIN

THE PLATE SPINNER CHRONICLES
Copyright © 2015 by BARBARA VALENTIN
Cover design by Estrella Designs

Published by Gemma Halliday Publishing
All Rights Reserved. Except for use in any review, the reproduction or utilization of this work in whole or in part in any form by any electronic, mechanical, or other means, now known or hereafter invented, including xerography, photocopying and recording, or in any information storage and retrieval system is forbidden without the written permission of the publisher, Gemma Halliday.

This is a work of fiction. Names, characters, places, and incidents are either the product of the author's imagination or are used fictitiously, and any resemblance to actual persons, living or dead, business establishments, or events or locales is entirely coincidental.

With love and gratitude to Marlene Kasten, the best plate spinning mentor this crazed working parent could have ever asked for and the best mom ever.

I'd also like to acknowledge Nancy Munson and Patricia MacMillan, my editors at the *Chicago Tribune*'s TribLocal, for giving my column a home. While I would never compare my writing to that of the late, great Erma Bombeck, these two working moms made me feel like I had come at least a little close.

CHAPTER ONE

I Spin, Therefore I Am

~ Welcome to My World ~

I'm a plate spinner. No, not the kind you might catch in Vegas or even on a rerun of an old variety show. In fact, my "plates" are not so much objects, but those elements of my life that get me out of bed in the morning faster than the promise of a hot cup of coffee.

With five boys and a full-time job, I have plenty of plates to spin. My "act," while not nearly glamorous enough for Vegas (and a little difficult to simulate on a stage), does seem to provoke the same sense of awe in just about anyone I meet who, on hearing that I have five boys, inevitably exclaims, "How do you do it?"

Before responding, I imagine an announcer's voice hushing the eager crowd in the audience. "And now, ladies and gentleman, the amazing Plate Spinner! Watch as she sets each of her plates in motion! See her dazzling display of making five peanut butter and jelly sandwiches while checking her office voicemail—*at the same time*. See how she unloads the dishwasher while dictating a shopping list to her *husband*. And, finally, home from a long day at the office, watch as she helps her kids with their homework *while making dinner!*"

The crowd roars with applause and the curtain parts. I appear, dressed impeccably in business casual with a mile-high showgirl headpiece, and go about spinning through a typical day.

I sigh at the millions I could be making in ticket sales and then soberly reply, "Oh, it's easy. They're great kids."

Welcome to the heady world of working parents. In some households, both parents work, and in some, just one parent works. In my case, it's me. After our third son was born, it only took a couple of months to realize that we were using our meager vacation day allotments to stay home with a sick child or two while watching thousands of dollars go to the daytime care and feeding of our three boys. We came to the inevitable conclusion—one of us had to stay home.

Careful and deliberate analysis over each of our career prospects, along with our individual ability to be a full-time caregiver to our children, yielded the obvious choice—my husband. It took about thirty seconds.

The relief I felt was instantaneous. No more stay-at-home mothers accosting me with comments like "I can't imagine paying anyone to raise my children!" No more having to endure raised eyebrows when requesting yet another afternoon off because a child had a slight fever. No more having to fly out the door by 5:30 to reach the facility before closing time so as to avoid additional "late" fees.

Does this make me a bad mother? Quite the contrary, it's a testimony to my wonderful, loving mother who worked full-time while raising us. She was a plate spinner extraordinaire. The one who taught me that plate spinning, a stress-inducing and largely underappreciated skill, is done by loving parents the world over whether they're at home or at work. No one had to fly to Vegas to catch her act either, but she would've totally rocked a showgirl headpiece.

~ Mom of Steel ~

"Able to leap tall piles of laundry in a single bound. On a conference call—look! It's a parent. It's a breadwinner. It's a Plate Spinner!"

OK, maybe I've spent too much time with my nose in my boys' comic books, but given the feats that I have to accomplish on a daily basis, I do fancy myself to be a project-managing, child-rearing, meal-planning, rule-instilling, errand-running superhero.

Greetings from Planet Suburbia!

OK, before my kids disown me, let me assure you that I'm not about to go traipsing around with a gigantic PS emblazoned across my chest and a way-cool glitter cape fluttering behind me as I go about my day. Instead, I'll offer up a list of my top five super powers.

  1. Backwards vision (aka, eyes in the back of my head)

All parents have it, but I wonder if they fully utilize its power. If you have your back to a child but can't hear them, they're up to no good. Count on it. A simple "stop right there" ought to spook them into submission.

  2. Time-shrinking

With some pre-planning—a concept that is foreign to children of all ages, you can reduce the time it takes to complete any task by as much as fifty percent. For example, if you were to get up at the same time as your child on any given morning and both had thirty minutes to get out the door, you could get ready for work, prep a nutritious dinner, check your email, and fix them breakfast while they're still scrambling to find two socks that match.

  3. Patience

Okay, yes, it's a virtue, but it's one of the most potent tools in your arsenal. Why? It enables you to endure just about everything your child can dish out, starting with grocery store temper tantrums when they're little to demands for tattoos and body piercing when they're older.

    4. Simultaneous Location Inhabitor (aka, S.L.I.)

You guessed it—being in two places at once. Note, there is a heavy dependency on technology for this one, as well as carpools, flextime and a *really* fast car with a fuzz buster on the dash.

    5. Stereo Babble Decipherer

The ability to actually hear two people talking at once cannot be underrated, especially for a busy parent. When both speakers are using the same tone—take, for example, a high-pitched dispute over who left the gas tank empty the last time one of them borrowed the car, it can take a while to pick apart exactly who is saying what.

My secret weapon? The Look. You know which one I'm talking about. Eyebrow arched, chin dipped, lips pursed? It renders its victims devastatingly polite. Before you know it, your kids will be relaying their thoughts, one by one, with perfect articulation and the utmost respect.

Now, go get your cape on—just steer clear of ceiling fans.

~ Happy Maternal Superhero Day ~

    Mother's Day is right around the corner and, while I'm tempted to parlay the gratitude of my husband and children into something sparkly for myself, I instead think of my own Mom, my plate-spinning mentor from Day One. Now in her seventies, I watch as she dotes on my boys and cares for my Dad, and find that I am learning from her still.
    Like her, I have five children and work full-time to help support my family. As the youngest of her brood, I had the benefit of witnessing her perform during her peak. By the time I came along, she was spinning plates like a pro, serving up square meals each night, doing the laundry, running evening baths, reading bedtime stories, crocheting ponchos for my Barbie dolls, and sewing Halloween costumes, all while forging a career for herself at our town's local newspaper.
    I'll never forget one particular night when I was in the second grade. After being tucked into bed, I woke up horrified that I had neglected to tell her that it was my turn to bring in cupcakes for our school's monthly Hot Dog Day. I rushed down to our laundry room, where I knew she was ironing, to drop the bomb. In reply, she flashed me a weary smile, told me not to worry about it and shoo'd me off to bed.
    Mystified by her calm response, I did as I was told, convincing myself that I would never have kids because they were way too much work. Nonetheless, in the morning, there they'd be. Perfectly-iced, homemade cupcakes tucked neatly in our handy plastic cupcake holder.
    For Mother's Day that year, I sauntered down to our neighbor's garage sale and slapped down a hard-earned quarter for a goofy little monkey statue that I was sure my Mom would love. That morning, she carefully unfolded the

paper from the comic strip section that I had used to encase her gift and acted as if I had gotten her a five-carat diamond, smiling, hugging me, and telling me that she absolutely loved it.

    Mission accomplished.

    From my childhood perspective, I thought it was normal for a Mom to take on the world. Right or wrong, my friends' mothers who stayed home all day didn't seem nearly as glamorous as mine. She did it all. She was my personal superhero who was wise enough to shift her cape around to her waist so she had something to wipe her hands on while cooking.

    This year will mark my sixteenth official Mother's Day, and while I've earned my share of beautiful, highly-cherished, handmade ceramic fish paperweights and Popsicle stick picture frames, I still marvel at all that my Mom did for us without the benefit of a microwave, email, cell phone, and store-bought cupcakes. While her cape has frayed a bit around the edges, she's still spinning her plates and even some of mine that would otherwise fall.

    So, here's to you Mom, my plate-spinning superhero—thank you for all that you do and all the love that you give. I don't know where I'd be without you.

~ *Releasing Your Inner Spinner* ~

Dear Plate Spinner,
I recently read an interview with Melinda Gates in which she discussed how she maintains her work/life balance. Does this make her a plate spinner?
Signed,
"Confused"

Dear "Confused,"
If a plate spinner is someone who is responsible for the care and feeding of someone other than themselves and they have to squeeze this responsibility in between another major obligation, like being a full-time employee or major global philanthropist, then yes, Melinda Gates qualifies as a plate spinner.

We may come in all shapes, sizes, and income brackets, but it's true. We are all striving for the same thing. Balance.

These tips, along with some practice, patience and caffeine—lots of caffeine, can help you achieve it.

1. Find a plate-spinning pal—A multi-tasking mentor to help you navigate the well-worn path to plate-spinning utopia, this person can be anyone whose skills you wish to emulate—someone who manages raising a family while excelling in their career, all with the cool precision of an Indy 500 race car driver.

For me, it was my Mom. For you, it could be anybody, but a word to the wise. Avoid looking to celebrities as role models. Their ginormous salaries aside, there is one thing they have that you don't—a staff (spouse and kids don't count).

2. Delegate, delegate, delegate—Speaking of spouses and kids, the wise plate spinner knows how to nurture and leverage the talent of her labor pool. If you have someone in your family who loves to cook, put them

in charge of meal planning and prep. Is someone particularly adept with computers? Perhaps they could start their own company, become wildly successful, attend G8 summits, and support you for the rest of your life.

Younger children, on the other hand, can be taught to take messages, dust, and water plants. Try to get them to do all three at the same time. It's never too early to start spinning.

3. Keep it real—Keeping the proper perspective will help you celebrate your successes and learn from your failures. Since there are only so many hours in a given day, keep your to-do list limited to what you can accomplish within that time frame. If your eyes are bigger than your plate-spinning capacity, your lengthy list will leave you feeling overwhelmed before you even start.

Ask yourself, "What's the worst that can happen if I don't get to everything I need to do today?"

So you end up serving frozen pizza twice in one week. Who cares?

You missed your daughter's recital to attend a budget meeting? It happens.

According to that interview, even Ms. Gates would agree—no one is perfect. Cut yourself a break every once in a while.

So, yes, "Confused." Melinda Gates is not only a plate spinner, aside from the difference in the number of zeros trailing her salary and mine, she and I are practically pals.

Oh, wait. I forgot. Celebrity...

~ Isn't Every Day Father's Day? ~

In the world of working parents, Father's Day looms large and, with it, the onslaught of store ads promoting ties, aftershave, watches and other gift ideas. My dear dad, now retired, believes that the third Sunday in June simply marks the culmination of Father's Day month, the kickoff of which falls, coincidentally, on Mother's Day—much to my mom's chagrin. Nonetheless, my dad is happy to receive a plate of his favorite homemade cookies and some new refrigerator art from my younger sons.

My husband's gift, however, requires more deliberation and planning. Memories of my mother whispering under her breath, "Isn't every day Father's Day?" echo through my mind briefly before they're pushed aside by a more recent image of my favorite stay-at-home dad, pulling a warm plate out of the oven for me when I arrived home after a long day at work.

As the day fast approaches, my mind begins to race. Gift buying is a plate I reluctantly spin because it must stay aloft until said gift is purchased. While gift cards offer a quick remedy, I have to remember that this is for the guy who, on more than one occasion, has gone above and beyond the call of duty.

Take, for instance, the time he nursed a couple of sons back from tonsillectomies while I had commitments at work, or the valiance he displayed when, during a recent trip to an amusement park, I backed out of a promise to ride with the boys in the front car of a new roller coaster, scary enough to prompt several warnings for the faint of heart.

These few examples, coupled with all of the limo driving, forgotten lunch/gym uniform deliveries, Band-Aid applications and hugs given, remind me that something much more special is in order. Like a new car.

As much as I'd like to do my part to bolster the auto industry, monetary constraints force me to set my sights on something a little more affordable. I confer with the boys. While my high-schoolers wholeheartedly endorse the new car idea, my younger two recite a list of video games that sounds vaguely like a rough draft of last year's letter to Santa.

When my only hope for inspiration appears to be window-shopping, I head for the door before getting intercepted by our middle son, the voice of reason amongst his siblings.

"I asked Dad what he wants." I admire his direct approach. My son continues, "The zoo."

Assuming my husband was suggesting a place for us to go so he could have some alone time, a holy grail of sorts for all harried plate-spinning parents, I agree.

"OK, sure. I haven't taken you guys to the zoo alone for a long time."

I beam at my spot-on deductive reasoning before he clarifies, "No, he wants us all to go to the zoo together."

"Really?" I close the door, somewhat perplexed.

Maybe my Mom was right—every day is Father's day.

CHAPTER TWO

A Plate Spinner is Born

~ Redefining Romance ~

Valentine's Day marks the anniversary of the day my husband and I got engaged. It also marks the day I started dabbling in the fine art of plate spinning. It began innocently enough, squeezing in a visit to a nearby bridal boutique on my lunch hour, but before long, I had crossed over to hard-core matrimonial multitasking, filling weekends with everything from reception hall tours to appointments with photographers, florists, and DJs.

By the time the next Valentine's Day dawned, our wedding was just two weeks away. Romance again beckoned, but with a blizzard blowing outside, this appointment-packed bride-to-be was left stranded with little more to do than count reception response cards.

While I looked forward to our life together, I somberly accepted the fact that our Valentine's Day celebrations would only go downhill from there. Marriage, so I had been told, would suck the very life out of our romance before we had even finished saying our vows. Maybe, just maybe, I'd get some flowers or the occasional box of chocolates. I figured, as time went on, I'd have to settle for a peck on the cheek and, if I was lucky, a card.

At the time, I thought nothing would ever top the surprise of seeing him get down on one knee in a crowded, candlelit restaurant, holding out a little black velvet box while popping the question.

That is, until our first son was born.

I woke up on that first Valentine's Day as a new mom feeling alarmingly well-rested. Venturing into our living room, I discovered why. With our infant son snuggled against him, my husband lay asleep in the recliner with an empty baby bottle at his side. As he heard me approach, he mumbled, "Happy Valentine's Day."

I believe I can speak for every working mother out there when I say that nothing says "romance" like being given the opportunity to get a good night's sleep.

Fast forward twenty years, one house, two careers, and five boys later, it's been my distinct privilege to be the recipient of a number of wildly romantic gestures that don't necessarily come on a particular February day, but to this non-morning person, are worth more than their weight in gold—like the hot cup of coffee that I find waiting for me when I have to start spinning my plates earlier than usual, or the one morning that I got up before the crack of dawn because I let my "fill-up-the-tank" plate fall to the ground the night before, only to find that he beat me to it. He had even popped in my favorite CD that started playing as I turned the key in the ignition. The memory of it still brings a tear to my eye.

And while I haven't received any additional velvet boxes with sparkly rings inside, my husband has gotten down on his knee for me since our engagement—never mind that it's been to tie my shoes when I've been too pregnant to find my feet.

~ Happy Valentine's Moment ~

While some consider Valentine's Day to be little more than a fabrication by greeting card companies, chocolate manufacturers, and florists to boost sales, a much less cynical segment of the population holds out hope for a glimpse of romance on this particular day. Not something to be rushed, the challenge for plate spinners falling into this group is figuring out how to squeeze it in.

Until my then-boyfriend decided to propose to me on Valentine's Day, I too was a cynic, manipulating more than one suitor to cough up roses and sparkly things because the date on my calendar said so. To me, it was just another day to hold my breath with the rest of my officemates when the floral delivery van would pull up outside of our building.

For this plate spinner, while time doesn't always permit for a staring-dreamily-at-each-other-over-a-candlelit-dinner type of celebration, the expectation for flowers and chocolates still stands. Getting some alone time with my husband, on the other hand, will likely have to wait until the kids are asleep—no small feat. Like herding cats, the bedtime routine in our house can be simultaneously invigorating and exhausting.

"Jammies and brush teeth!" I announce, just loud enough so all can hear.

Like clockwork, the older two obediently run up the stairs to get ready for bed. The next two in line typically act as if they didn't hear me and continue with whatever they're doing. The youngest meets me somewhere in the middle. Fond of walking around bare-chested, even on frigid winter nights, he ignores my requests to don a shirt while categorically refusing to brush his teeth.

When I repeat, "Jammies and brush teeth!" just loud enough for our neighbors to hear, my fourth son is spurned into action. He puts his PJs on and joins his father in front of the television to see the sports segment on the news. After reminding him where he can find his toothbrush, I go to our upstairs computer and IM my son still sitting at our downstairs computer, "Jammies and brush teeth. NOW." I hit the Return button. He replies, "In a minute..." I reach over and unplug our home network.

"Mom!!"

The impact of his feet stomping up the stairwell can be picked up on earthquake monitors in Los Angeles.

With the last one on his way to bed, I get the coffeemaker ready while my husband, updated on all things sports, pulls a cork-topped bottle from the refrigerator. It's finally quiet. Tension begins to roll off of my shoulders as he turns on some Easy Listening music and pours a couple of glasses of wine.

Snuggled on the couch, we clink glasses, yawn and call it a day.

~ Getting Carded ~

I don't know about you, but I was in kindergarten the first time I got carded. No, apple juice wasn't a controlled substance back then, and no, I wasn't on a liquor run for my parent's New Year's Eve party (besides, my feet wouldn't have reached the pedals).

It just so happens that's when I received my first Valentine's Day card.

I still remember the thrill of tearing open the tiny envelopes to see which of my peers addressed one to me. It didn't matter that we had been instructed in advance to bring enough for the entire class. What mattered the most was whether the object of my secret crush gave me one that said "Be Mine" instead of "Pals 4 Ever."

But, by third grade, the excitement over getting a little piece of cardboard with Batman's picture on it saying something like, "Blamo! You're the greatest!" had lost its luster. That was probably about the time that my Grandma turned me onto chocolate-covered cherries, a gift my Dad would give her each year, and I've been hooked ever since.

I didn't get carded again until I was in college and, again, it's not what you think. Finding a big red envelope waiting for me in my dorm mailbox on Valentine's Day was almost better than getting flowers or chocolate. Almost.

But here's the best part—because my husband-then-boyfriend filled every speck of white space inside of it with heartfelt sentiments, sealed it in an envelope, and trusted it to the United States Postal Service for delivery, I still have it. It's sitting right here in my keepsake box, ready to be pulled out and read again whenever I want to relive the moment, or remember how I got into this plate-spinning mode in the first place.

Don't get me started on ecards. Even if it comes with a personalized message, animated or not, there's little romance to be had in clicking a button to open a file. While convenient, they're not perfumed or adorned with ribbons and can't be stored in a keepsake box unless, of course, you print it.

Be still my beating heart.

And, while email has its merits, speed of delivery being chief among them, no amount of emoticons can make up for the lack of a handwritten, sentimental expression. Taking the time to actually select, address, and mail a card leaves the recipient with a snapshot, frozen in time, of your affection for them.

My husband has probably forgotten all about that first Valentine's Day card that he sent me eons ago, but I'm sure if I ever decide to exploit the contents of it for my own personal gain—say for a new kitchen, I bet he'd remember.

It won't be long now before I take my youngest to the store to pick out Valentine's Day cards for his class party. Maybe for the last time. He is, after all, in the third grade.

CHAPTER THREE

Spinning from Home

~ Working From Home Rules ~

Telecommuting. For most breadwinning parents, the very word conjures a vision of a perfectly balanced lifestyle, one in which work and home are seamlessly intertwined.

I'll be the first to admit that working from home is not without its advantages. Experience, however, has taught me that if kids are about, the line dividing work and home can quickly become blurred.

To help redraw the line, we have a list of mutually-agreed-upon rules to keep the two straight.

1. If my office door is closed, do not open it. Ever.

On a recent frantic morning, one of my sons alerted me to the fact that his supply of clean underwear had been depleted. Throwing a quick load in the wash, I ascended to my office to prepare for a mandatory cannot-miss, must-participate-in meeting with members of my project team. Just as we were diving into the gritty details of said plan, my son burst in with, "Hey Mom, the underwear's done!"

"Great... Thanks, honey," I replied after hitting the mute button on my phone with enough force to push my car down the driveway and onto the street.

2. No singing in the shower.

Because my home office shares a wall with my sons' bathroom, and the members of my project team do not appreciate the aesthetics of Top Forty hits as much as they do, singing in the shower is banned when I am on the clock.

3. Dazzle me with your survival skills.

Remember that despite being home, I really am working. The last thing I want to see when I punch out is a sink full of dirty dishes. Also, do not expect me to fetch things, make things or clean things that you can fetch, make or clean yourself.

4. No electronic devices at the kitchen table.

Why? They're distracting, cause disputes over possession, usually emit whirring, beeping, or vroom-vroom noises, and divert one's attention from the meal.

In short, playing with toys at the table is just plain rude.

As soon as my husband reminded me of this, I closed my laptop and slipped it into the briefcase sitting innocently at my feet.

5. The planner does not leave the office.

Arriving late to a lovely sit-down dinner with my family, I took a head count and noted that all were in attendance. No one was at Scouts, track practice, or the library.

We had a quorum.

So, while everyone was enjoying their food, discussing their day, and telling newly-learned jokes, I pulled out my planner and, knee bouncing furiously under the table, started running through my agenda. Topics included: family vacation ideas and a review of open action items ("Honey, where are we at with getting that check engine light diagnosed?" and "Didn't I ask someone to shovel today?").

Something in their blank stares told me that I had crossed the line.

Perhaps this rule is in need of an edit.

5. The planner *notebook* does not leave the office. The planner in me, however, is allowed time off for good behavior.

~ *Playing Dress Down* ~

Maybe it was the plaid wool uniforms I had to wear to school during my formative years. Maybe it was the hand-me-downs I was forever inheriting from my older sisters. Maybe it's because the only time I played "dress up" as a kid was on Halloween. Or maybe I inherited the I-Hate-Shopping gene that runs down the male side of my family tree like a polka dot tie on a striped shirt.

Whatever the reason, I spend an inordinate amount of time staring at the contents of my closet each and every morning, wondering what to wear. Not exactly time well spent for this busy plate spinner.

Until someone comes up with a line of mix-and-match separates for grown-ups, I tend to wear a lot of black, grey, khaki, and red. My fashion-savvy sister, on the other hand, is always decked out in this season's latest styles and colors. She inherited the I-Love-Shopping gene from our mother whose affinity for apparel acquisition was rivaled only by Leona Hemsley. When my parents moved to Phoenix, Marshall Field's went out of business. Coincidence?

I don't think so.

Luckily for me, though, my closet floor is cluttered with shoes my sister has tired of. If only those white slingbacks went with anything dangling from the rod above them, I'd be in business. As it is, I trod through my day clad in either my running shoes or, on dressier occasions, my black loafers.

I admit it. I find fashion daunting. Where style may not be as much a priority as comfort and cleanliness, I suppose there is some truth in the saying that clothes make the person. Yet, the whole idea that apparel can transform me from just another slipper-wearing, bed-head coifed adult to a power-suited, designer shoe sporting, top-notch executive is transparent at best. Having delivered my share of presentations with a baby formula smudge on the padded shoulder of my newly-purchased $400 suit, I can assure you that it only takes one oatmeal-smeared good-bye kiss to poke a hole in your charade.

While my executive presentation days may be behind me, fashion still dictates which role I'll play on any given day. Take this morning, for instance. I wanted to wear something that would make me feel confident, creative, and entrepreneurial. The image of the late Steve Jobs, former Apple mogul and the idol of my tech-savvy sons, came to mind.

Reaching for my black mock turtleneck shirt and blue jeans, I effectively turned the game of "dress up" on its ear and it's working like a charm. I feel a revolutionary product announcement forming in my head as I write this. I haven't a clue what it will be about, but with what I'm wearing, I'm prepared to walk in front of a packed house of media reps and investors, eager to hang on my every word.

I can only hope my kids are in attendance.

~ Tools of the Trade ~

No matter what your occupation, there's no denying that plate spinning is an indispensable skill for parents, both in and out of the workplace. Yet, without the proper tools, we'd be left stumbling around with phone numbers written up and down our arms, strings affixed to our fingers, and little yellow pieces of paper stuck to our foreheads, reminding us of all of our "to-dos."

As great conductors use batons to create one harmonious sound from several disparate sources, we must utilize some type of instrument to keep things humming along smoothly. At work, you might have a wide array of options at your disposal, all designed to give you the illusion that you're in control of your time—everything from sprawling spreadsheets to computer-based calendars to sleek, savvy smart phones that beep at us when we're supposed to hurry along to the next thing.

Wherever we go, we can remain connected to our schedules, obligations, and contacts. And, like death and taxes, upgrades to these products quickly render the version we have just mastered obsolete. While some of these upgrades are truly improvements (how many of you remember the boxy computer monitors sporting a black screen with bright green print appearing as you typed?), I think I'm speaking for plate spinners everywhere when I say that flashier and more expensive doesn't necessarily mean "better."

Thankfully, at home our tools can be far less complex. In my bustling household, our paper-based tool of choice is a large desktop calendar that hangs on our kitchen wall. Each child is assigned a different color marker that is then used to chart each of their activities. Yes, this method harkens back to the Stone Age when Neanderthal plate spinners were still chiseling their to-do lists on cave walls, but it remains elegantly simple.

Yet, just as computer companies "up-rev" their products, over time, we've had to enhance our system. For instance, "Release 1.1" came out after our third son started preschool. In the interest of space, it became paramount that all entries be written both legibly and accurately, and we switched to fine-tipped markers. The next major enhancement came out when, after adding two more boys, we needed the option to highlight entries in yellow if more than one child was involved in any given activity. And, after our two older boys started high school, we upgraded to the long-anticipated "Release 2.0" enabling the highly-touted pencil/eraser capability.

As each month passes, I peel off the multi-colored mess. Before the gleaming white page has me searching for my sunglasses, I take a deep breath and quickly begin filling in family birthdays, anniversaries, and national holidays. School events are next—concerts, athletic events and field trips. When I'm done, I step back to admire my work. While still theoretically simple, in reality, one page of our calendar could easily earn a spot on the wall at the Museum of Contemporary Art. Especially during the school year.

Looking down at my rainbow-splotched hands, I write one last entry for the day—"Research Release 3.0, the paperless version."

~ Banking On Time ~

If time is money, then being granted an extra hour of free time is akin to winning the lottery. No one knows this better than plate spinners who, on a daily basis, must adhere to a strict time-based budget just to make it through the day.

Managing the two commodities is strikingly similar. For money management, simply balance what you earn against what you spend. Pay yourself first by allocating a percent for savings. Know that the IRS is going to pocket a portion for taxes, but you might get some back in a refund.

The payoff for properly managed dollars? Zero debt and a hefty rainy day fund.

Time management is similar. I balance twenty-four hours against the time needed to complete my daily task list. I pay myself first by allocating eight hours right off the top for sleep. I know that Daylight Savings Time is going to pocket an hour each March when we "spring ahead," but I also know that I'll get it back each fall.

The payoff for properly managed time? Zero to-do's and a good night's sleep.

Monday through Friday, my tasks are usually predictable, so my time budget is relatively fixed. The weekends, however, are similar to a futures market. Like a harried trader, I try to anticipate what impact things that are largely out of my control will have on my schedule, like my boys' social lives and homework loads.

If I were to take the analogy a step further, I would liken an emergency fund to a good night's sleep. In that scenario, things like stress and insomnia, like the cost of unanticipated car repairs, can quickly deplete my account.

Compounding matters is the fact that my time-based account is usually in the red when the weekend arrives. Like a person who uses credit to purchase items instead of saving up for them first, I sometimes commit to things knowing full well I don't have the reserves to cover the cost and I dread the day the balance is due.

For me, that day is usually Saturday, my day off. It's the day that should be obligation-free, but rarely is. Things like housework, grocery shopping, and cooking from scratch all come due. With interest.

It's no wonder, when I think of the extra hour allotted us each fall, I feel that same giddy excitement that washes over me when I find forgotten cash in an old coat pocket. Unanticipated, it's not targeted for anything obligatory like paying bills. Therefore, depending on the amount, I can use it to splurge on anything from a lottery ticket to a big bar of imported chocolate bliss—either way, a treat.

The same holds true for that extra hour. Unanticipated, it's not targeted for anything obligatory like chores. Therefore, knowing the amount, I can use it to splurge on anything from sleeping in to snatching some quiet time with the Sunday morning paper—either way, a jackpot.

~ The Dreaded "B" Word ~

Impending deadlines aside, when forecasters announced that a "potentially life threatening" blizzard was headed our way, my first instinct was to rush to the store. Like a football player with the ball tucked securely in the crux of his elbow, diving over a mass of bodies huddled on the one-yard line as he tries to make a touchdown, I threw myself into the crowd fighting for the last cart.

Elbowing my way around the greedy shoppers, protecting my kitschy clutch like a coveted game ball, I made a beeline for their well-stocked supply of chocolate. I smirked as I watched the others scurrying through the aisles, stocking up on more sensible supplies like bread and meat.

As I approached the mob at the checkout line, the harried cashier took one look at my measly purchase and pointed to the end of the line located back by the freezer section. After several minutes of enduring the glares of other parents, their carts overflowing with enough food to last them through Memorial Day, I thought it best to blend and threw some milk and eggs in my cart for good measure.

Normally, this little excursion would've taken me fifteen minutes, tops. Two hours later, I arrived home with my stash.

Was it worth it? Let me put it this way—there was no way, on God's white earth, that I was going to weather this snowflake tsunami without a little cold cocoa comfort.

My boys, on the other hand, had a different reaction entirely. As soon as they heard the "B" word, my younger two crossed their fingers and toes, hoping that school would be cancelled. The older two were more skeptical. They've had their hopes dashed before.

For the record, this plate-spinning telecommuter has mixed feelings about snow days.

On one hand, a day off for the boys means that I don't have to worry about making lunches and getting them to and fro. I can focus on my job that I am blessed to be able to do from my home office. The only interruption in my day would be shouting out rosters for the rotating shoveling shifts.

On the other hand, there would be the inevitable interruptions to help with boots and snow pants, dole out hot chocolate, and ensure that they spend at least some of their newfound freedom on studying a bit.

Still, every single weather authority agreed that we were in for a winter wonderland version of Armageddon.

So confident was I in their forecasts that I didn't even plan to set my alarm for the next morning. I just knew that I would be awoken by the velvety voice of our school district's superintendent, informing me of the cancellation.

Next time, though, I'll have to remember to ask him to keep a door unlocked for me at one of the schools so I could get my work done there... I'd even be willing to part with some of my chocolate for the privilege.

CHAPTER FOUR

A Chip Off the Old Plate

~ Textin' 'Bout My Generation ~

  According to AARP, this is a big year for me. Just as I was about to take out an order of protection against their multimedia membership onslaught, I learned that it would get me a discount at all sorts of stores and restaurants like IHOP.
  Sweet.
  I can accept the fact that I have a milestone birthday to look forward to (I'd wink, but my crow's feet are resting right now). I can even accept the fact that I am probably one of the oldest moms on the playground when I retrieve my youngest from school. It's when I attend a function at my boys' high school that I begin to feel downright rickety.
  Physical differences aside, looking out over the crowd after a recent band concert, it was obvious—the only real difference between my generation and the one that's coming up in the ranks is body language.
  Many of my peers, I noticed, were huddled in groups, making eye contact, conversing, and laughing. I could tell they were enjoying each other's company because they were saying things to one another like, "It's so good to see you!"

Many of the students, on the other hand, stood alone, off to one side, heads down, still, and silent. Their thumbs, however, were moving at lightning-fast speed.

Yes, I'm generalizing and yes, I know that many adults enjoy texting and have the over-developed thumb muscles to prove it. I'll carefully climb down from my soapbox (lest I break a hip) now, but I do worry that the younger generation would struggle far more with a widespread power outage than my generation would.

In fact, last summer we lost power when a squirrel ran out of luck on a power line. About thirty seconds passed before my kids piled in the car and bolted into town, hoping to find a place to plug back in. My husband and I chose to light a candle and take advantage of the peace and quiet to indulge in the luxury of having an uninterrupted conversation.

And I know I'm not helping matters when, like my parents before me, I tap into the shock and awe value inherent in stories from my youth—especially the ones that shed a light on just how far technology has come since my pre-TV-remote childhood.

In my day (there I said it; you knew I would), I had to get up and change the channel if I wanted to see a different show. Being a material girl, I asked my parents for a typewriter, not a laptop, when I headed off to college. Music came on flat vinyl disks that I bought at a record store and I remember when MTV actually played videos, 24/7.

While my generation managed to survive in an Internet- and app-free world, it's hard to say if the younger generation is better off. I suppose they'll have the answer by the time their kids ask them what it was like to grow up with old-fashioned things like an iPod Touch or a Wii.

Now, if you'll excuse me. If I'm going to make the early bird special at IHOP, I'd better scoot.

~ Color Me Embarrassed ~

Parenthood.

No other job on this planet holds such rich potential for hide-under-a-rock embarrassing moments. Between the lack of sleep, overwhelming amount of activity day-in and day-out, and the major shift in priorities, the opportunities are endless.

I think I speak for mothers everywhere when I say that it all starts in the delivery room.

In the throes of labor with my firstborn, feet high up in the stirrups, while doing my best to cut off the circulation in my husband's hands, I'll never forget watching in horror as a parade of interns walked into the room to observe my son's entrance into the world.

OK, so maybe that's a little beyond embarrassing and fathers don't have much to counter with, but still—my sense of modesty? Poof. Long gone.

After that, I truly (and naively) thought I was beyond embarrassment. Showing up at work with formula stains on my clothes did little to turn my cheeks red and arriving to pick my son up from daycare with the zipper open on my khakis only prompted me to laugh and shrug.

But that was all before my second son, button-pusher that he was back then, made the call—THE call—to 9-1-1.

While I was in the shower.

"Mommy! There's a man at the door!" my oldest cried as he knocked on the bathroom door.

"Is it Daddy?" I called out. Not getting a reply, I shut the water off, squeezed the water out of my hair, wrapped the towel around me and tiptoed to an upper-level window where I caught a glimpse of someone with close-cropped black hair.

Breathing a sigh of relief, I flew down the stairs to the front door. Figuring my husband had forgotten his key, I flung the door open wide.

As my eyes took in the sight of the tall, not unattractive, fully armed police officer standing on my doorstep, I pulled the towel tighter across my chest and did my best to smooth my mess of tangled, wet hair. My only hope was that the crimson in my cheeks brought out the color of my eyes.

"Can I help you, officer?" I asked with all of the dignity I could muster, noticing a smirk twitch at the corners of his mouth.

"Did you call 9-1-1, ma'am?"

"Uh, no!"

Leaning toward me, he glanced around.

Maybe it was the small pile of little light-up sneakers in the corner. Maybe it was the menagerie of stuffed animals strewn on our couch. My guess, it was the giggles that finally erupted from the top of the stairs that prompted him to ask, "Ma'am, do you have toddlers in the house?"

"Yes." I shot the offenders a look that silenced them instantly.

"May I have a word with them?"

Heh, how the tiny are fallen.

"Boys!" I shouted. "Get down here."

After reading them the riot act about only dialing 9-1-1 in emergencies (and, no, your brother not letting you play with his toys did not constitute an emergency), he bid me adieu.

Since then, my dignity has for the most part remained intact and my modesty is none the worse for wear.

Knock on wood.

~ Wagon Rides and Jaguar Dreams ~

Yes, I'm a plate spinner with a relatively large family, I live in the suburbs and some of my children even play soccer, but no, I do not drive a minivan. When the size of our family grew from four to five, my husband and I knew we needed something bigger than our two-door hatchback, but we were reluctant to go with the automotive flow. Recalling fond childhood memories of snagging a coveted seat in the "back back," waving and making faces at cars driving behind ours, and having our parents yell directives back to us as if we were in another room, we set our sights on buying a station wagon.

Unable to find anything resembling the gas-guzzling behemoths of our youth, we downsized our expectations and took a smaller version for a test drive, not so much to see how well the engine would enable us to peel out of the daycare center on our way to work, but to see how well it could accommodate the three different types of car seats our boys were using at the time.

Sitting comfortably in the front seat, my husband and I caressed the clean blue vinyl dashboard and spotless carpeting on the floorboards. Unlike its flashier minivan counterparts, boasting options like multi-CD shufflers and side view mirrors that lit up when the turn signal was engaged, we happily settled for this little wagon's special features—two handy cup holders and a rear-window defroster.

Flash forward ten years and the car that our children initially referred to as "neat" became one that they were loathe to accept a ride in, fearful that they'd be spotted by anyone they might know and pitied by the rest. Our oldest, on the cusp of getting his license, reluctantly agreed to accompany me on some errands. While it seemed like just last week that he was sitting in the backseat enjoying

Cheerios and apple juice, he reflexively sank low in the front seat as we pulled up to a stop sign.

Glancing out my window, I spotted it. In the lane to my left sat my dream car—a hunter green Jaguar with tan leather seats. Excited, I pressed the "down" button for my window, forgetting that it had stopped functioning years before.

Seeing me struggle, the driver of the Jaguar looked at me with a politely inquisitive look on his face as if to say, "What is it, my dear woman?"

Realizing that I would be unable to verbally relay my appreciation of his car's aesthetics, I simply mouthed, "Love your car!"

I then smiled winsomely and drove on. Looking in my rearview mirror, I saw the driver frowning and slowly shaking his head, mouthing "Wacko!"

I glanced down at my son, who had slithered onto the passenger side floor, his face now crimson.

"Are you OK?" I asked innocently.

He glared at me and climbed back into his seat. "Tell me we're getting rid of this car soon!" was all he said.

"If I had a dime for every time you said that, I could've bought one by now."

And, again, I apologized for being minivan repellant.

~ Licensed to Survive ~

Despite our superhero aura, we working parents are mere mortals. Still, if I had to choose one superpower, I'd pick the ability to be in two places at once. Between job schedules, errands, and familial obligations, my life would be so much easier if only I could somehow physically co-locate myself.

But, until some evil genius develops this ability, I'll have to keep relying on Plan B—granting my child permission to drive. Despite watching a large chunk of my hard-earned paycheck go towards financing my auto insurance rep's vacation to Hawaii, having an additional driver in the house has proven to be an indispensable tool in my plate-spinning arsenal.

While ushering my two older boys into the licensed population, I rode shotgun on my fair share of white-knuckled excursions. When my life was not flashing before my eyes, I managed to jot down the following pointers:

1. Driver's Ed—Public School or Private Company?

In most communities, there are two driver's education venues—public school curriculum or private companies. Compared to private instruction, taking it through their high school may not necessarily be a money-saver, but here are a few things to consider:

— The duration of the program—most states' requirements for new drivers cannot be crammed into a six-week long program offered by many private companies, but fit nicely within the confines of a semester-long schedule.

— The timing of the program—if your child is involved in any sports or other extracurricular activities, taking driver's ed during their school day—instead of after school or on the weekends, may work best. If your child balks about having to take driver's ed during the school day, remind them that it might just get them out of taking PE.

Note: Whichever venue you choose, you are still on the hook for helping them meet your state's minimum drive time requirement prior to obtaining their license. If you play your cards right, this could take years.

2. Deflect Attention

You've seen them—cars with "student driver" stickers plastered on the rear window. As if it's not embarrassing enough for them to make thirty-seven-point turns or come to a hard stop twelve feet before they get to the stop sign, why humiliate them further by advertising the obvious to surrounding, possibly hostile, drivers? The level of tension in the front seat is already escalated enough without it. As such, ditch any "student driver" sticker you were planning to affix to your rear window.

3. Mind Your Reflexes

How you react during practice drives will have a major impact on your student driver, affecting not only their self-esteem, but your safety as well.

Whether they are nervous and skittish or overly confident and careless, just remember:

— Stomping on an invisible passenger-side brake will not make the car stop any faster.

— What sounds like words of encouragement to you (e.g., "slow down," "stay off the shoulder," and "garbage cans aren't for target practice") can sound like screaming to your child.

4. Drive the Talk

The key to producing a safe driver is modeling safe driving techniques. Aside from the usual no-no's—texting, eating, or reading the paper while you're driving, proper technique is just as important. The last thing you want is a dirty look from your child's driving instructor after hearing that you taught them how to bank a turn using nothing but the palm of one hand or even an elbow.

And there you have it. Good luck and Godspeed (just remember to stay within the posted limit).

~ Riding on Vespas with Joy ~

Back before kids, before careers, before even spinning a single plate, my husband (well, technically boyfriend at the time), used to buzz around Chicago on his vintage Vespa—a refurbished model, single-seat, 1950's turquoise with shiny chrome trim that was originally orange, of all things. It didn't really go much faster than thirty-five mph, but it was perfect for city living.

During the day, my pre-hubby would use it to get to his job on Michigan Avenue, hoisting it up onto the curb and chaining it to a nearby parking meter. At night, I'd hop on the back and we'd zip around Downtown, Uptown, Old Town, and Lincoln Park, visiting with friends, going to the beach, the zoo, and art fairs, hanging out at neighborhood taverns and coffee shops afterwards.

If we wanted to pick up a pizza and stay in for the night, instead of losing my coveted parking space, we'd hop on the Vespa and I'd sit on the back, balancing the pizza on my hip with one hand, clutching my pre-hub with the other. Even the mundane task of grocery shopping was made a little more cosmopolitan by simply donning some Audrey Hepburn shades and pulling up to the Jewel on our way cool Italian scooter.

It just didn't get any better.

Then we got married and started a family.

And moved to the suburbs.

When we rolled the Vespa off of the moving truck, it looked woefully out of place in the land of vinyl-sided split-levels. As if it knew. I could almost hear it whispering, "We're not in Old Town anymore." Out of respect, we tucked it into a cozy corner of our two-and-a-half car garage.

That was nearly seventeen years ago and, I'm sorry to say, I haven't given it much thought since. Unlike a mint-condition black Vespa that we spotted on a recent trip to Rome, ours is now dust covered, having endured years of neglect. Teddy bears have assumed the driver's seat, while boxes of old books and, gulp, albums have been stacked on top of it.

Our boys have often asked about the hunk of motorized metal sitting abandoned in our garage. In response, we smile and regale them with stories of our carefree days living in the city, riding up and down Wells avenue or Clark street. Just going for joyrides.

They scratch their heads. Joyrides? What the heck are those? I clumsily try to explain the term used for traveling about with no intention of having to be anywhere by a particular time, or buying anything from any particular store, or running any errands of any kind. Just taking in the view, the people, the sights and smells of the city.

Huh.

I truly had forgotten all of that, busy as I am with five kids, two jobs, and a husband. Rides, many. Joy, zip.

My husband and I recently moved our oldest into his dorm in the Windy City. After he was settled, we decided to grab a bite to eat and found ourselves back on Wells. Happy to have found parking, we chose a restaurant and seated ourselves at a table with a street view.

The memories came flooding back. Our son rolled his eyes as we pointed to establishments that had been there back when we were residents, recalling memories of going here and there. And we would've gladly spent the afternoon as such until our son slapped us back into the moment with one short inquiry.

"Hey, about your old Vespa..."

~ Autism's Upside ~

Depending on how you choose to look at it, plate spinning can be both stressful and fulfilling. Even on her most hectic days, my Mother chose to stare down stress with a "glass half full" optimism that enabled her to tackle any challenge that came along. As the youngest of her five children, I created many of these challenges, especially when my siblings would accuse me of being her spoiled-rotten favorite (although the entire universe knows it was really my brother).

Mom would blithely mediate any disagreements by airily reciting, "You're all unique and I love you all the same." She said it so often, I wondered at times if she really meant it.

These days, I hear myself reciting these same words to my own children, not to quiet accusations of favoritism, but to let them know that I truly love each of them because they are so very different—an especially potent message for our boys because one of them happens to be autistic.

Born with beautiful curly hair and sparkling eyes, we knew from the onset that he was different from the rest. It wasn't until he turned two, and was not yet speaking, that we learned just how different he would be. At the urging of his pediatrician, my husband and I arranged to have him evaluated by a specialist.

At our appointment, I heard myself reasoning, "He has three older brothers. Of course he doesn't speak. He can't get a word in edgewise." Nonetheless, we watched as the clinician observed him and attempted to interact.

Within ten minutes, she blurted out the diagnosis as casually as if she were reciting her food order at a drive-up window. "He's got autism coupled with sensory integration issues."

We promptly enrolled him in an early intervention program and moved on with our lives, rejoicing in even the smallest achievement. We quickly discovered, however, that others decided to go the "glass half empty" route.

Well-meaning observers would try pointing out things like his aversion to crowds. I'd smile and counter, "He's a Libra. What do you expect?" When he had difficulty coloring or trying to write his name, I'd remind anyone within earshot that he is left-handed, the only one of my bunch.

Nine years and several stellar teachers, therapists, and support staff later, our son has gone from being a non-verbal, eye-contact-averse, wheel-spinning toddler to a very verbal, smart, happy, soon-to-be sixth grader. Being a member of a plate-spinning household has also served him well. While we may be short on time, we are long on routine—a necessity for those affected by autism. And, by virtue of living in a house with a wide age range of siblings, his social skills are tested and honed daily.

Conversely, there are times when we must stop spinning our plates long enough to view the world through his eyes. What we see is an entirely different universe that's sometimes worrisome, often no different than ours, and usually nothing short of wonderful.

If you can look beyond the way he sometimes speaks too loudly, gets too close, or hugs too tightly, you won't find a more loyal, generous, and kind spirit.

Is he my favorite? They all are, of course.

~ Music to My Ears ~

Modern day plate spinners have highly evolved survival skills. Generations of parents have toiled in the workforce while raising their families. Ultimately, this has resulted in our ability to simultaneously use all five senses to accomplish superhuman feats like making it through the day in one piece. How else would we be able to negotiate video game privileges with a bored child over the phone while texting a message to a colleague as we're watching a web-based presentation during which we pick up the acrid scent of popcorn scorching in our office microwave just in time to savor the taste of the few remaining bits that didn't burn?

Technology aside, the same holds true at home. Next time you're seated around your kitchen table at dinnertime, pay attention to the way in which you use your senses. Can your taste buds detect if anyone has slipped sugar in your saltshaker (or vice versa)? Do you watch to ensure that the vegetables you dished out are actually making into your children's mouths instead of their napkins? Does your nose pick up the smell of rolls burning in the oven while your ears register the sound of the smoke detector going off? Did you feel that kick on your shin that was mistakenly delivered by one child but meant for another?

In my world, sensory overload is a common occurrence. Sometimes it stressful, but on the upside, it gets the blood pumping. And, while I can usually spin right on through it, one of my sons absolutely cannot manage it. He has Asperger's Syndrome, a form of autism.

When my son was diagnosed, my husband and I were told that he would never blend seamlessly with his peers. Undaunted, we made his continued improvement a goal. With the support of behavioral specialists, we focused on increasing his tolerance to sensory stimulation, helping him build an arsenal of coping mechanisms to get him through situations that he finds stressful. Fortunately for him, dinnertime at our house provides the perfect opportunity to hone his newfound skills.

Sitting at the table with his four siblings, it's not uncommon for several conversations to be going on at once. The noise level naturally escalates as each person strives to be heard. And, as the boys have grown, our once enormous kitchen table has become increasingly snug, especially for my son—our only "leftie."

We had an opportunity to gauge just how far he has come at a recent family celebration. In the past, when we would dim the lights, bring out the cake, and break into a chorus of "Happy Birthday," he'd clasp his hands to his ears and run from the room crying (not unlike my reaction to turning forty). On this particular night, however, he joined right in, loud and clear.

Now that's music to my ears.

~ Running with Asperger's ~

It's not easy being the younger brother of three cross-country athletes—especially when you have Asperger's Syndrome (often referred to as "high functioning autism").

But, such is the case for my fourth son.

Eligible to join the cross-country team at his middle school last year, he did try it. Once. After that first practice session, he was unable to shake the self-imposed pressure he felt to perform.

Eager as we were to have him tread in his older siblings well-heeled footsteps, we recognized that he just wasn't ready.

"Maybe next year," we thought and hoped.

Relieved, he immersed himself in his classes, thriving in the well-structured environment that his support staff, themselves bursting with expertise, compassion, and rigor, provided.

With that school year behind him, like his peers, he looked forward to summer break—a time to recharge his batteries. His oldest brother, though, had other plans, seizing the opportunity to "get some miles on his legs." Hitting either the local college track or the local nature path just about every day, son number four steadily increased his endurance, if not his speed.

Before we knew it, we were restocking school supplies and meeting new teachers. And again, we raised the possibility, asking our son if he would like to give cross-country a go.

After much hand-wringing, he reluctantly agreed. When we assured him our only expectation was that he do his best, even if that meant finishing in last place, he readily agreed.

The season got off to a quick start. After only two practices with the team, he found himself lining up with the rest of the sixth and seventh grade boys at his first meet. Not sure what to do with the strange mix of nervousness and excitement that he was feeling, he stood twirling a curl that hung at his forehead—his current soothing gesture.

We hung back, hoping for the best, and watched as the first clump of boys darted past in a blur.

"Where is he?" we wondered. My first thought was that he pulled himself out of the race. I hiked the video bag over my shoulder and was about to set out to find him when we saw him making the first turn, shuffling along. A relieved laugh escaped me. There he was—the little engine that could.

Lap after lap, same thing. The first clump would rush by and several minutes later, he would amble by. Alone.

At the finish line, the fastest blew through, victorious. One by one, the rest followed, winded and sweaty. With much of the last lap hidden from view behind trees and bushes, we were left to wait and wonder. Where is he? Will he finish?

We didn't have to wait long. In the distance, we saw the red sleeves of the T-shirt he had worn under his jersey, ever so slowly coming closer.

As he approached the shoot, the cheers started—not just from us, his parents and little brother, but from other parents and members of his team who had already finished.

Maybe it was the physical exertion. Maybe it was the sudden attention. Or, maybe it was the yelling that to him, unable to discern the emotion behind it, was just too loud. Whatever it was, it brought tears to his eyes as he crossed the finish line. His official time hovered right around twenty-five minutes. He didn't see the smiles that were big enough to crack our cheeks. He didn't see our own tears that we blinked back as he approached.

He just wanted to go home.

After he cooled down, though, it began to soak in. He did it. He ran a race and he finished. Maybe running wasn't so bad after all. Maybe he wasn't so different after all.

Every race since then, his time has improved substantially, clocking in at just over seventeen minutes for his last finish.

So thanks to his coach and all of the adults and friends who have cheered him along this season. The difference you have made in this young man's life is one that will endure the test of time.

CHAPTER FIVE

Don't Sweat the School Stuff

~ Back-to-School Countdown ~

Flipping the family calendar to August invariably triggers a chorus of groans. And not just from my boys. While they have school to look forward to, I get to celebrate the fact that I am one year closer to getting that AARP membership. Oh joy.

While not especially thrilled at the timing of my birthday, I did snag some unusual gifts. Take, for instance, the year I got two new white uniform shirts and a forty-eight-count box of Crayola crayons. Not exactly the new Partridge Family album I wanted, but still.

At the time, I thought my mom had it in for me, but now I see the genius in her plan. Combining a birthday with school supplies was just more evidence of her master plate-spinning prowess. If I had any doubts about her motives, she would cleverly distract me with a beautifully decorated bakery cake. Man, she was good.

Since my boys' birthday's fall everywhere but August, and I don't possess anything close to my mother's dizzying multitasking capabilities, I am left to my own devices. Here, then, is my countdown to school.

4 weeks before—If you have student athletes, make sure all of their medical forms are up-to-date. If not, many urgent care clinics can do sports physicals, but may charge

more. In a pinch, try convincing your child to try out for a spring sport instead.

3 weeks before—If your child is in need of a new backpack or lunch bag, start looking now. Chances are, if you wait, your son may be stuck with "Hello Kitty" slung over his shoulder and your daughter will be forced to have lunch with the likes of Hulk and Bob the Builder. In any event, look forward to their middle school days when you can ditch lunch bags for brown bags and their backpacks become design-free.

2 weeks before—Print off your child's supply list from their school's website and get shopping. Granted, these items can be pre-purchased as a fundraiser in some districts, but for those of you who like the thrill of the hunt, now is the best time to take advantage of office supply and discount store sales. Remember to plan wisely, though. Gas prices being what they are, what you may save in getting a five-cent Pink Pearl eraser at one store may not be worth having to drive across town for the two-dollar pencil box to put it in.

1 week before—Take your kids in for haircuts now to avoid that "new-haircut" look on their IDs and in their school pictures. It's sweet when they're young, but just not cool when they're older.

1 day before—Forget about school and focus on enjoying the last day of summer break with your kids. Splash around in the pool with them, grill their favorite foods and challenge them to a firefly-catching contest before bed. They're not getting any younger, you know, and neither are you.

~ Fall Fundraising Fiasco ~

Like construction trucks in the summer, bright yellow school buses can be the bane of a commuter's drive. Try as I might, I inevitably get stuck behind one as it darts in and out of rush hour traffic. OK, maybe "darts" isn't the right word. Perhaps "lumbers" would be a better fit.

Nonetheless, if it weren't for the fact that I have school-aged children, the appearance of buses is a sure sign that school is back in session.

But, just in case you missed it—perhaps you take a train to work, are able to work from home full-time, or happen to work on a remote space station, there is another surefire way to tell that the new school year has started—fundraisers.

You won't have to look far to find this clue. It's probably lying in wait in your office kitchenette right now, ready to pounce.

You'll walk in, innocent, your mind fuzzy from inhaling school bus exhaust fumes on your way into work. Groping for the coffee pot, you'll see it—a brightly-colored order form taped to the cabinet door, directly at eye level. You'll squint, noticing a little yellow sticky note affixed to it. Reading the rushed, but legible, handwriting, you'll discern that no child could've written it. But it doesn't matter. The message is clear.

"Please, please, please buy these candy bars, cookies, popcorn, kitchen gadgets, magazine subscriptions, or (in my case) wrapping paper to support my child's school, sports team, scout group, band trip, or other extracurricular activity."

If you read between the lines, you can also see, "My child's happiness, self-esteem, and ultimate fulfillment of their destiny on this planet—along with their ability to earn cool prizes like limo rides or pizza parties, is riding solely on your willingness to fork over some $$$."

No pressure. On the contrary, everyone knows that there is an unspoken quid pro quo rule in the world of fundraising that often belies office politics.

Stressed and still caffeine-free, you realize you have two choices: 1. You can whip out your checkbook, pour your coffee and toast your own generosity or, 2. You can look the other way, vowing to pick up some Starbuck's on your way into work the next day, cursing your coworker's attempt to parlay your hard-earned dollars into funding a good cause.

It's your choice.

Sure the kids aren't doing the legwork, but as a working parent of school-aged, fundraising children, I must admit that the last thing I want to do after working all day is walk them door-to-door for donations.

Besides, why in the world would I subject them to the sting of rejection inherent in signs that read, "No soliciting" or in comments like, "I gave at the office."

Taking my child's fundraising packet, I slap a sticky on it with my name and office extension, and shove it in my briefcase.

I just hope he saves a spot for me in the limo. Whoops, there's the doorbell. Gotta go!

~ *College Countdown* ~

Facing the glass door that separated me from the high school counselor's office, I tapped on it, smiling politely. When she looked up at me and frowned, I knew she had no intention of letting me in. Beginning to panic, I spoke loudly through the glass. "I'm sorry, but my son is scheduled to meet with a college representative tomorrow. There must be some mistake. He was in Kindergarten just last week!"

"What?" my husband mumbled, in bed beside me, squinting at the time flashing on our alarm clock before dozing off again.

Wide awake, I lay there trying to replay the past twelve years. Had I not been so busy spinning plates, maybe I would've been better prepared to face the fact that my oldest child was several short months away from leaving the nest. Not one to wallow in regret, with all of the college visits, applications, personal essays, and meal plan choices facing him, I decided there was no better time for him to test-drive his own plate-spinning skills.

Since attending a college fair, my son is getting more mail than Santa at Christmas. Rifling through the brochures, however, does little to facilitate his decision-making process. With the ACT registration deadline beginning to take shape on his horizon, my husband and I suggested that he pick a handful of colleges to see in person. After carefully checking his schedule, he registered for several open houses, some near, some far—all squeamishly expensive.

We tossed him a brand new plate emblazoned with "Apply for Scholarships."

The first open house we attended was at my alma mater, a downstate campus he's visited before while accompanying us to homecoming games and relatives' graduations. After hearing the Admission Director's presentation, visiting with the academic representatives within his area of interest, and peering into an actual dorm room inhabited by a real live college student, he was sold. No need to look any further. This was where he wanted to go. Whew! What a relief, I thought.

Then came the next open house.

At a completely different campus, my son quickly became enamored by the newer dormitories, historic buildings, and proximity to downtown. This, now, was where he wanted to go. Well, good, I thought. All part of the decision-making process. How about one more, just for comparison's sake? Reluctantly agreeing, he chose a small private college nestled in the suburbs. Approaching the day with a less-than-rosy view of the place, he joined a campus tour led by a vivacious upperclassman named Kristi. By the time the tour was over and we were enjoying the complementary catered lunch under lovely white tents situated in the middle of their diminutive "quad," he was busy re-shuffling his choices.

At our high school's "senior parent night" last Spring, the counselors recommended that incoming seniors have three to six schools to which they would want to apply come September. That way, they reasoned, when the college representatives come to visit, they can be sure to introduce themselves. I think he'll be ready. And so will I.

~ The "FAFSA" Shuffle ~

If "Fill out the Free Application for Federal Student Aid form" looms large on your to-do list, then you are old enough to have college-bound children. And you're old enough to remember "The Hustle," that disco classic that had us poking our fingers in the air as we danced the night away, probably wearing way too much polyester. Or, so I heard—I was just a child at the time.

While having filled out this form only once before hardly makes me a veteran of the process, I highly recommend keeping this upbeat tune in your head while gathering up your prior year's W-2, bank statements, and other pertinent material. Unlike "It's a Small World," at least "The Hustle" has a good beat and you can dance to it.

I know of which I speak. The college application process has tested my plate-spinning mettle before. Coming through it relatively unscathed, I thought I was ready to start it all over again with my second son, now a high school junior. Like any good second child, he is the opposite of his older sibling in more ways than I can count. If it weren't for the comfortably familiar bureaucratic financial aid form and standardized testing applications, I would indeed be in foreign territory. Yet even these cannot shield me from the great unknown that is my second son's future.

Before starting his college hunt, my oldest had specific search criteria in mind—a mid-sized university that offered a diverse liberal arts-minded environment, located within a three-hour radius from home, and boasting a reputation for cranking out top-notch teachers. On the other hand, son number two's only requirement is that the campus be outside of the Midwest. Beyond that, it's anybody's guess.

In his defense, he's a busy guy, focusing on becoming the proverbial well-rounded student. Working off of a lesson I learned the first time around, universities seem to crave them with much the same appetite I had for blueberries and root beer while expecting him. These mythical creatures do it all—ace the ACT/SAT, rank high in their class, excel in extracurricular activities, serve in their community, and soar high above the clouds wearing a red cape and tights.

Pardon the exaggeration. On closer examination of the fine print, I see that tights are optional.

It's no wonder he doesn't have time to consider the choices before him. My son, studying hard for entrance exams and his advanced classes, is a year-round athlete, a talented musician, and a soon-to-be Eagle Scout. His plate-spinning skills put mine to shame. And he's doing all this just to get the opportunity to spend thousands of dollars for the next four years; after which, he'll walk away with another diploma and a monthly loan payment he can count on receiving for years to come.

At least he'll have a mini-fridge and maybe a futon couch to show for it.

Still humming that old disco classic? Good. Now, get on your dancing shoes and do the FAFSA!

~ The Ties Have It ~

What's a seven-letter word that starts with "b" and ends with "e" and is something every plate spinner needs to succeed? You guessed it. B-A-L-A-N-C-E. It's the one thing that you can't spin without, but achieving equilibrium is an ever-elusive goal.

This was most evident to me when I watched my son head to the tuxedo rental store recently. Clutching a swatch of fabric from his prom date's dress, I knew that he was about to spend roughly the same amount for the rental that his date did for her dress which, by the by, she gets to keep.

Need a six-letter word for the one thing that can knock balance off its feet?

C-U-S-T-O-M.

If I were to turn this prom-prep custom on its ear, girls would be the ones rushing to dress rental stores, clutching one of their date's ties, hoping for the perfect match. Silly, I know. But, I am tempted to ask that my son's date take one of his ties with her before she goes dress shopping for the next big dance. He does have plenty from which to choose.

A dear friend of mine, and mother of two lovely high-school aged young women, is quick to remind me that the girls have expenses of their own for which they, too, must shell out big bucks—the hair, the nails, the jewelry, and the shoes, just to name a few.

Put in its proper perspective, this formal affair can be considered a bit of a pre-wedding primer. With the exception of the rehearsal dinner and maybe a box of toothpicks for the hot hors d'oeuvres, the cost for weddings traditionally falls on the bride's parents. Again, custom thumbs its nose at balance.

To avert this, my then-fiancé and I chose to take matters into our own hands. We decided the kind of wedding we wanted, got estimates on everything from photographers to DJs to florists, then set the date based on how long we figured it would take us to save up for it. One year later, we hand-delivered a check drawn from our joint savings account to the reception hall of our choosing that covered the cost of a lavish reception for a hundred of our closest family and friends.

Striking this balance, we not only maintained control over the details, but we got to test drive our plate-spinning abilities while we planned it, drew up a budget, and stuck to it. We had the time of our lives with none of the debt-induced aftertaste typical of large expenditures. Truly a life lesson.

As for prom, the focus for both genders should be to have the time of their lives, not an evening spent tallying up a scorecard of expenses.

In the end, I'd call it a tie.

~ Financing Prom 101 ~

Dear Plate Spinner,
Prom is an expensive but socially important rite of passage for teens today. What are your ground rules? And how do you keep costs in check?
Signed,
Parent of a Prom Date Wannabe

Dear P.P.D.W.,
While I take exception to it being classified as "socially important," I'll focus instead on the expense of prom by posing this question: If students were mandated to self-finance their attendance at this formal affair, would the whole notion of it fade into a strobe-lit sunset?

When my son announced that he asked his girlfriend to prom, he was quick to point out that he and his date were going to "go Dutch" on the tickets. Whew, what a relief, huh?

Given that one ticket to the event runs close to what I recently forked out for a new dishwasher, I informed him that if he wanted to go, he would have to pay for it himself. To support his efforts, I handed him a well-timed coupon that had just arrived in the mail from a formalwear shop along with a lengthy list of chores that, on completion, would help fund the purchase of his date's corsage, a haircut, and a car wash. I can only assume his date's parents would follow suit, suggesting that she do whatever possible around the house to help finance her ensemble and a trip to the salon—like install new siding on their house and repave the driveway.

If you haven't figured it out by now, I did not go to prom. My first big formal dance was my wedding reception. The two events are not without their similarities. In both, the couple puts out big bucks to look their best.

And while my son's date gets to keep her dress, just like I got to keep my wedding gown, after the event was over, I got to keep my date, too.

As for keeping the cost of prom in check, if you want to go, instead of sticking your parents with a hefty credit card bill, why not earn what it would cost to go before hand?

Now that's my idea of a socially important rite of passage.

~ Gifts for Grads ~

While filling out invitations for my oldest child's upcoming graduation party, the proactive plate spinner in me sprang into action. I asked my son, who had only just recently lost his hard-fought battle against senioritis, if he had a gift wish list—should anyone happen to ask.

"Well, I need a laptop," he ventured.

"Yes, and I need a vacation in the south of France," I thought to myself before delicately suggesting things of a more practical nature, like a laundry basket or a travel iron.

He rolled his eyes and left me alone with the guest list and memories of my own high school graduation.

Despite heading to different universities, my friends and I were only interested in getting the three T's—a typewriter, a turntable, and a trunk (on which to set said turntable). That, along with a plank of wood and a couple of crates (in which to store our albums), and we would have the equivalent of the modern-day entertainment unit right there in our very own dorm rooms. The vision of it had us excitedly cruising the back lots of fast food places hoping to snag matching plastic milk crates that, we were disappointed to find, only seemed to come in white or black.

In those pre-information-age days, we also had the added thrill of not knowing who our roommate would be until move-in day. Not a big deal, really. We were accustomed to speaking to other people face-to-face or, if need be, on the phone. For me personally, having shared a bedroom with my two sisters, coexisting with just one other female, I figured, would be a walk in the park.

If you can remember a world in which iPods and MP3 players didn't exist, then you can understand why a major source of concern for my friends and I was whether the stranger with whom we would be living shared our affinity for Peter Frampton, Journey, and Supertramp. A worst-case scenario, we imagined, involved being forced to share the cozy confines with someone who had brought along their collection of opera classics or any of that new icky punk rock stuff. I remember adding "headphones" to my wish list and hoping for the best.

When I did finally learn the identity of my first-ever college roommate, I remember being thrilled to learn that she was not only bringing her brand new electric typewriter, but was willing to let me share it if I would supply the carbon paper and Wite-Out.

My son's return snapped me back to the present.
"Hey, how about gift cards?"
"From which place?" I asked.
He rattled off the names of his favorite eateries.
Now it was my turn to roll my eyes. "I've got two words for you—meal plan."
Then I wrote, "Your presence is the only gift needed" at the bottom of his invitations.

CHAPTER SIX

Home Is Where the Plates Are

~ Home Sweet Money Pit ~

The description in the paper read, "Cute split-level farm house, professionally decorated and landscaped."

Looking back, I wasn't aware that a degree in creative writing was a prerequisite for a real estate license.

I saw the house and its newly planted *For Sale* sign jutting out of the snow-covered lawn on my way home from work. The realtor agreed to meet my husband and I that very night to take a look at it.

With her fur coat and rhinestone covered fingers, the listing agent had all the air of a self-promoted local celebrity. When she blithely referred to the property as a "perfect starter house just loaded with charm," I knew we were in the hands of a pro.

After passing through the lime green and yellow-sponged foyer, the first stop was the kitchen. Squinting out of the window over the sink, I gasped. From what I could see of the dimly lit .79 acre lot, the back yard had a deck, a patio, lots of mature trees, and was fenced all around.

What I couldn't see at the time was that, while the professional landscapers may have actually stepped into the yard at one point, they hadn't been back for years. Not even a Christmas card.

Taking one look at the dining room's busy floral wallpaper that sported colors not seen since before

Madonna debuted on MTV, I had to ask, "Exactly how many years ago was this house professionally decorated?"

Much to our realtor's chagrin, we turned up the lights in the living room. It appeared as if someone had taken a stencil to the walls, leaving dusty rectangular imprints where previously hung pictures had been.

Still, we needed a house and this one fit the bill and our budget. We plunked down twenty percent, certain that our realtor would make a beeline to the hardware store with her cut to buy more twenty-watt bulbs.

Two weeks after moving in, our boys, both under two at the time, developed bronchitis. At the same time, the furnace choked out its last warm breath.

Inspecting the filter that was covered with a thick compacted layer of dirt, the HVAC repairman said nothing, but handed my husband a card for a duct cleaning company. It was a wonder we all weren't coughing up a lung.

Perfect starter house loaded with dust...

One new furnace later, we had our ducts sucked out and settled in.

Giving the boys a bath in the upstairs tub a short time later, my oldest asked, "Mommy, why is it raining inside?"

I glumly recalled the same inspector who had given the furnace a "thumbs up" joking that he was sure the house had a roof; he just couldn't see it under the foot of snow that covered it.

New roof. Check.

Thank goodness we had that professionally landscaped yard to stand in as we watched the roofer flick off shingles with the dexterity of a Vegas card dealer.

We didn't mind the big expenditures then, thinking we'd surely get some of it back when we moved on.

That was just over seventeen years ago.

Since then, we've replaced the water heater (twice), the air conditioner, the windows, the siding, the garage doors, and the insulation, and have repainted nearly every single square inch of the interior at least three times.

Imagine our delight when, this spring, we noticed the shingles on the south side of our roof beginning to curl at the edges. It has also come to our attention that we can do a better job cooling the house than our A/C unit simply by exhaling after eating popsicles.

It. Never. Ends.

Maybe the time has come to put it up for sale. Rotten real estate market notwithstanding, I think some lucky young couple out there would love to get their hands on a perfect starter home just loaded with charm.

~ *My Junk Drawer Runneth Over* ~

Raised in a household in which both parents worked, my live-in grandmother cared for my siblings and me. A loving taskmaster, she had us all help with the housework. Early on, I was assigned the arduous task of pulling the blankets on my bed all the way back up to my pillow when I got up each morning. Once I mastered that, I was handed a dishtowel and relegated to the kitchen so I could dry dishes after dinner. Although still height-challenged, I played the "I'm-too-short-to-put-them-away" card on more than one occasion.

Nonetheless, with three adults and five kids crammed into a modest one-bath ranch, clutter was often a point of contention between my parents. My dad did not believe in keeping anything. As soon as newspapers were read, they were banished to the recycling pile from which my mom would ultimately retrieve them, hoping to someday have time to clip articles of interest and the occasional recipe. In the meantime, the stacks of rainy day reads grew like paper-based high-rises in the corner of one closet or another.

Seeing nothing wrong with this, she was once quoted as saying that clutter was the reason God invented closets.

"One man's junk is another man's treasure," was also a favorite saying that she borrowed from her own mother, my Nana.

Whenever we visited Nana, I made a beeline for her kitchen and pulled open the last drawer on the right because I knew that's where she kept all sorts of cool stuff—an old wooden yo-yo, little bottles of bubbles, an old skate key, jacks, card games, and all of the factory rejects my grandfather would bring home from his job at Tootsie, a local candy factory.

I balked when I heard her refer to this in-kitchen treasure chest as a "junk drawer" until she assured me that all of the best homes had them.

In that grand tradition, the first thing I did when we moved into our house was proclaim the handled pullout space between the oven and the pantry door as our official junk drawer. I christened it with a stray cough drop and a used Pink Pearl eraser.

Seventeen years later, it is stuffed with things like empty thread spools (might need them for a school project), used corks (that can double as bobbers and pin cushions), and things like old wall plates, stray screws and tools for pumpkin carving, a plastic clothes pin, and a replacement bulb for a chandelier that is no longer with us.

Not a treasure in sight.

Diving in to search for a much-needed paper clip or safety pin would likely fill an entire afternoon. The time had come to oust the junk. It took me five minutes.

After pulling out the drawer and dumping the contents into an empty box, I slid it back into place. Sealing the box, I asked my husband to deposit it in the garbage can for me.

Sorry, Mom, but I'm going to have to side with Dad on this one.

~ Conquering Garage Envy ~

Dear Plate Spinner,
I dread this time of year. Every Saturday, all of our neighbors have their garage doors open because they're either doing yard work or having a yard sale.
Their garages are so clean and organized. My garage, on the other hand, is a cluttered mess.
My husband and I both work and our teenagers, between school, lessons, and practice, are always busy. I'd love to be able to actually pull our cars into the garage, but I'm afraid we'll never find the time to declutter.
Will I ever see my driveway again?
Signed,
Bursting in the Burbs

Dear Bursting,
Not to worry. By following these simple steps, you'll have a garage that your neighbors will envy.
1. Tap your in-house work force.
If you have older children, you're in luck. If you have a high school-aged child and they're attending prom, you lead a charmed life indeed. Several weeks back, when my son announced that he was going to ask his girlfriend to the dance, I immediately suggested that he clean out our garage to help offset the high price of the affair. It may be just another high school dance, but it is one at which formal attire is de rigueur and the cost of attending roughly equals that of a down payment on a Chevy Malibu.
2. Buy a shed.
These little one-room units come in a broad range of styles, shapes, and quality. Some are wood. Some are plastic. All of them will afford you a place to put bulky items like lawn mowers, snow blowers, fertilizer spreaders,

and the hammock your husband claims he got just for you on Mother's Day ages ago. But, I digress...

3. Get giant suspension hooks.

Imagine if you will giant hooks affixed to the ceiling of your garage from which you can hang things like bikes, rolled up tents, and your college-aged child's laundry when they bring it home on break and expect you to clean it. You'll be amazed at all of the floor space that suddenly opens up.

4. Have a garage sale.

Purchase a sheet of little round stickers. Write numbers on them ranging from .50 to five in whatever increment you care to. Walk around your garage, randomly affixing a sticker to each item left standing. Poke larger objects first. If they are breathing, they're likely a member of your family or a household pet and are, therefore, not for sale.

5. Ditch the rest.

When your garage is just about empty, look around and see what's left. See the old paint cans, the half used bag of charcoal that was left out in the rain because you thought your husband had brought it inside but he thought you did, and the broken scooter that you planned on fixing, but when you finally got around to it, your child had their driver's license? Drag them to the curb, slap a garbage sticker on each and call it a day.

~ *A Stitch in Time* ~

After a long day of slaving over a hot laptop, I had no sooner collapsed on the couch when one of my sons stood in front of me, holding a pair of his Boy Scout uniform pants.

I looked up at him. "No thanks. Olive green isn't a good color for me."

Without missing a beat, he informed me that they were too short for him. "And we have to leave in ten minutes."

When I didn't respond, he shook them at me. "Please?"

I looked over my head to see how I could've missed the large flashing sign that read *Seamstress—Needs Work*.

"Mom, just adjust the pins so they're longer." With that, he dumped them in my lap and I tried to figure out what he meant by the strange "pin" reference. On closer inspection, the memory came flooding back. It was a similar night, three years earlier, when a shorter version of this same son pulled on a pair of new, un-hemmed pants and, in the interest of time, I pulled out a box of safety pins and adjusted the length.

That I completely neglected to go back and properly hem them came as no surprised to my husband. He learned early on in our marriage that if he wanted a button sewn on any of his clothing, he would have to do it himself. After years of walking around with bandaged fingertips, he finally gave in and enlisted the services of our dry cleaner.

Unlike my mother before me, sewing is a plate that I refuse to spin. Maybe it's because I remember her spending night after night hunched over her old Singer machine, making my sisters and I everything from matching culottes, Easter dresses and Halloween costumes, to elegant bridesmaid dresses. Or, maybe it's because I have all boys. Whatever the reason, in my house, if it rips, it gets replaced, not repaired.

For like-minded plate spinners, I'm thinking that Scouting organizations ought to publicize the sewing requirement before accepting membership fees from parents of eager would-be Scouts. The uniforms constantly need adjusting as the Scouts progress through their program. And then there are those stiff little circles of appliquéd fabric backed with dried glue that parents are somehow supposed to affix to their kids' sashes and shirts with a needle and thread. Whoever came up with that idea must be behind those flimsy hangers on which my husband's shirts hang all pressed and lightly starched. I'm sure of it.

If it weren't for my dear mother, willing and able to sew these badges on my sons' shirts and sashes, I'd have no choice but to send them to the dry cleaners.

Hey, wait a minute…

If you'll excuse me, I've got some pants to pin—I mean, hem. I sure hope we have Band-Aids.

~ *Delegating Dilemma* ~

A couple of weeks ago, I issued an appeal for innovative, non-PB&J lunch ideas for my sons' brown bag lunches. I'd like to thank all of the plate spinners out there who generously responded with suggestions ranging from ham and cheese tortilla wraps to cracker sandwiches to mini-subs. All ideas were greeted with enthusiasm by my boys because none of them required peanut butter, and by myself because each item is easy enough for them to make on their own. As a mother of all boys, this supports my mission of raising self-sufficient future plate spinners—something I hope my future daughter-in-laws will one day appreciate.

While lunch making is one chore that I delegate without pause, at the beginning of any given weekend, I always have a lengthy list of tasks that must be completed in order to keep our household humming along smoothly. However, future daughter-in-laws notwithstanding, there is one chore that I am reluctant to delegate.

Laundry.

Pre-children, laundry was a chore that my husband and I tended to when we ran out of clean clothes. We could go for weeks, if we had to, without doing a single load. Then came our first child. Initially, we were shocked to discover that this tiny infant's new wardrobe could fill the industrial-size washing machine in the apartment building we were living in at the time. We barely had time to recover before being stunned by the frequency with which we had to clean said wardrobe. Short of laminating his clothes, we had no choice but to do more frequent loads.

Since becoming homeowners and adding four more boys, we are on our third washing machine, upgrading to a larger capacity with each replacement. And, with each upgrade, the settings have become more sophisticated.

Where our first machine boasted two cycles—hot and cold—our current model provides touch screen options for choices such as "jeans" and "cotton kitchen rugs" (not to be confused with cotton bathroom rugs, apparently).

Logic suggests that such sophisticated features would enable even my first grader to run a load of laundry without turning a load of whites into a load of pale blues. Yet, it only took one harried morning trying to find a white blouse that had not been rendered pale pink or gray, for me to realize that providing more options does not necessarily guarantee that the correct one will be chosen, especially if the items were not sorted correctly to begin with.

Since my idea of unwinding at the end of a busy workday does not involve anything having to do with a bottle of detergent, for my own sanity and that of my future daughter-in-laws, I am in need of a solution to this dilemma. Short of posting a simple workflow diagram above the hamper in our bathroom or using color-coded laundry baskets, I am open to ideas.

~ Pastel Green Persuasion ~

The recent Fourth of July weekend held much promise for this plate spinner. With my husband and older boys out of town for a 10k race, aside from the obligatory parade and fireworks with my younger sons, the family calendar was as empty as a golf course during a thunderstorm.

I made the mistake of mentioning this to my sister who is known in more intimate circles as the "DIY Diva." Her ability to transform the dreariest of dwellings is admirable, but her powers of persuasion are the stuff of legend. If she'd been given the opportunity, she could've sold a tube top to Coco Chanel. She's that good.

After my last brush with a can of paint, I vowed that I would never tackle the task again. But, like labor pains, the memory fades. In five short minutes, she managed to convince me that the yellow walls in my kitchen had faded to a dreary beige, the sponged walls of my foyer predated poodle skirts, and the wallpaper in my bathroom was recently seen in an episode of *The Brady Bunch*. On returning home, I wondered how in the world I could have subjected my family to such horrid conditions.

Before I knew it, while the country was awash in red, white, and blue, I was stuck inside, taping trim and covering the inside of my house with the so-not-patriotic colors of key lime pie and pistachio pudding. It's no wonder I spent the better part of the weekend fighting the urge to rush to the store for a can of whipped cream.

Instead, the only store I visited—several times as a matter of fact—was the home improvement store. Oh, and that reminds me. I'd like to give a shout out to the guy who recommended that I apply two coats of custom-color, non-returnable paint before deciding whether it was the shade I had in mind (you go, Gary!). And who knew little sponges on sticks provided better coverage in tight corners than a brush? I also discovered on one of my many trips there that, when trying to avoid getting oil-based primer on the leather-lined steering wheel of my car, I can drive just as well with my elbows. It's a wonder I don't just ditch this whole writing thing and take up professional house painting.

With the outdoor temperature and humidity level registering in the upper nineties, my sister and I worked in an air conditioned, but largely unventilated, environment. I expected the headache, but really didn't remember ever liking the oldies station so much. Good thing it came in loud and clear on our bathroom radio. And good thing our windows were closed.

The job is done, the paint has dried and I have to admit that my house looks mighty fine. Now, if I could just get Gary to take me up on my recommendation to install a cooler filled with cans of whipped cream in his paint department.

It would've saved me a trip.

~ Seasonal Clothes Shuffle ~

At the beginning of my working parent tenure, with a little practice, it didn't take long before I was reveling in the reliable rhythm of my routin—sleep, go to work, make dinner, help with homework, sleep, go to work, make dinner, help with homework. You get the idea. Once I had that pattern humming along nicely, I was able to enhance it into something a little more complex—sleep, take a shower, go to work, make dinner, help with homework.

While practice makes perfect, some things that still throw me for a loop are the plates that only require occasional spinning—like holiday decorating or school supply shopping. After one of my older boys heralded the arrival of Spring this year by heading off to school wearing shorts and flip flops (the temperature was, after all, over forty degrees), I let out a heavy sigh, realizing it was time for the dreaded seasonal clothes swap-out.

Even as an infomercial played in the background, singing the praises of giant plastic bags into which you can allegedly stuff your entire closet, suck out any trace of air, and be left with a bag flat enough to slip through the mail slot in your front door, I scoffed and lugged out our giant plastic bins that were ready to burst with my family's warm weather clothing.

After years of doing this, I have a practiced plan in place.

Certain that I had stored the clothes by size last fall, I instructed each boy to gather their winter items, bring them to me and I would exchange them for a bin containing the same-sized summer items. Once they deposited their summer items in their drawers, they would return the empty bin to me and I, in turn, would transplant the winter items and tuck the bin back into storage. Simple. Shouldn't take more than a few minutes, I reasoned.

Like a quarterback, I huddled them around me and quickly briefed them on my strategy. I ignored the skeptical glances they exchanged with each other as they headed off to their respective rooms. Instead, I sat with a smug smile plastered on my face as I listened to hangers scraping along closet rods and dresser drawers being pulled out.

Within minutes, I was surrounded by sweaters, long-sleeve shirts, jackets, mittens, scarves, and all manner of long pants, wondering how I could've neglected to tell them "one of you at a time, please."

As I worked my way through the heaps of clothes, I opened the first bin. Perplexed, I asked no one in particular, "OK, why does this just have shirts in it?"

By way of reply, the boys began claiming theirs. I watched, stupefied, as they opened the remaining bins and dug out their shorts, bathing suits, and summer pajamas. Within minutes, my family room looked like a textile mill had exploded.

Several hours later, I collapsed onto the couch. The boys' summer clothes were neatly folded in their drawers and hung in their closets. The winter clothes that had survived the season were stored away in the bins. A large bag, filled with items too small for my youngest, sat in the corner, destined for the next charitable pickup.

I groped for the remote, hoping to catch the local weather forecast and heard, "Possibility of record-breaking cold."

CHAPTER SEVEN

Holiday Plates

~ Halloween Costume Countdown ~

    It is with no small amount of regret that I've come to accept that in just a few short years, Halloween will be a very different experience for me. Gone will be the days when I rush to catch the costume parade at my youngest son's school, then stroll the neighborhood with other parents as we watch our trick-or-treaters scramble from one house to the next. Before long, I won't have to referee any intense candy trade negotiations between my boys, breaking them up when they turn ugly.
    Perhaps most regrettably, I'll miss being able to confiscate any and all chocolate after convincing them that it was all part of a national recall.
    Since I can't imagine any other use for green glow-in-the-dark skeleton gloves or a battery powered Buzz Lightyear wing jet pack, the big bag of costumes that we've accumulated through the years will be relegated to a closet, forgotten. And what a waste that would be. The polyester ghost costume that has seen better days now looks truly spooky. No longer bright white, the purposely frayed edging is downright ghastly.
    All in all, that bag must contain a dozen or so costumes of varying sizes that were brand new when I got them for my older guys and well worn by the time the younger ones were done with them. And yet, I just can't

bring myself to donate or give away this bag of memories. Not yet, anyway. I'm sure my youngest will soon be foraging through it looking for this year's selection. Loathe as I am to plunk down my hard-earned cash for a new costume that will get limited use, I wonder if I could talk him into wearing the same dinosaur suit that he wore in preschool. Since much of his arms and legs would now be sprouting out of it, I could pitch it to him as an archeologist-eaten-alive-by-a-dinosaur costume. Not sure if he'll bite.

Maybe I'll just rummage through our closets. There are scores of abandoned sports uniforms—everything from soccer to karate outfits. If he takes a pass on those, maybe one of my husband's old suits, rolled up at the arms and legs, would do the trick. If all else fails, I could wait until the night before when my adrenaline levels spike and I come up with some truly scary costumes like "Crazy Colander Head" or "Vacuum Attachment Boy."

If only I'd inherited my mother's love of sewing (and her sewing machine to go along with it). Despite having a full-time job, she stayed up late on many pre-Halloween nights creating the most lavish and well-crafted costumes for my sisters and I, including, but not limited to, princess gowns with lots of itchy crinoline, furry pink bunny suits, and Raggedy Ann and Andy frocks. Seeing us in the finished product would leave her beaming. These days, seeing me sew on a button leaves my guys speechless.

Oh, I've got it! How about the Ghost of Buzz Lightyear Meets the Green Skeleton of Doom? Wait...I'm pretty sure he wore that last year.

~ Thanksgiving Grace ~

In my plate-spinning world, if preparing for Thanksgiving were an Olympic event, my sisters and I would be gold medal contenders. Drawing a stark contrast to our childhood when we sat across the table arguing over who would get a coveted drumstick or who had more whipped cream on their pumpkin pie, we learned long ago that we work better as a team.

As she did back then, our mother tries to calmly remind us, "It's not about the food." My sister Mary, the one who studies cookbooks like a new parent does Dr. Spock, respectfully disagrees.

We appoint her our unofficial captain.

After we reach a consensus on both the venue and the menu, she delegates who's bringing what and when. Each of us does our part, trusting that, when the day comes, everything will be perfect. And, with the exception of any conflicts arising over who has to sit at the dreaded "kiddie table," which way the food should be passed, or whether it's too early to be playing Christmas music on the radio, it usually is.

If you are fortunate enough to find yourself surrounded by family and friends this Thanksgiving, before you dig into your sumptuous feast, take a moment to remember that, as self-sufficient as we like to think we all are, we are not invincible. At some point, we all need a helping hand. Not convinced? When's the last time you treated a child's broken bone all by yourself, or helped one master a math concept that you yourself had long-ago forgotten?

This holiday season, before you set out to tackle another busy day, beginning every sentence with "I have to," take a moment and think about all of the people behind the scenes who help us along without any expectation of thanks or recognition. Teachers, clergy, coaches, and neighbors.

Before you put so many plates in motion that you fool yourself into believing that the whole world revolves completely around you, think about those people who are always there when we need them, willing to put their lives on the line for us, yet we rarely give them a second thought. Firefighters, police officers, doctors, nurses, and those serving in the military.

Before you find yourself having to walk over plates that have crashed to bits around you, stop and think of the people close to you who may be in need, but know better than to ask. Your friends, your kids, your parents, your spouse.

You get the idea. I'm sure you can think of more examples of people without whom your plates would come crashing down faster than you can say, "I appreciate everything you do."

So, during this holiday season, don't just say grace, show it. Instead of worrying that your gravy may have too many lumps or that your dressing may be too dry, slow down long enough to spend some face time thanking people who matter.

And remember, it's not about the food. Really.

~ An Ode to Thanksgiving ~

'Twas days from Thanksgiving, and nothing was done
My job needed effort, my kids wanted fun.
The deadlines at work kept me stuck in my chair.
Leaving no time to shop or plan with care.

A large crowd was coming to eat on that day.
The nieces and nephews and in-laws would stay.
A ball game they'd watch on my flat screen TV
Eating my pie and cheering with glee.

The thought of the crowds, wanting nice food and fun
While projects at work kept me under the gun
Had me wondering why in the world I would host.
When all I want is to sleep in the most.

My work must come first, I cried and implored.
I have to do well ne'er my job be off-shored.
My sisters assured me they'd come to my aid
Leaving all doubt behind that I wouldn't get paid.

"Rally the children to help with the cleaning
Surely they can't spend the day just IMing!"
My husband, so wise, had me in fits of laughter.
Just wait, I told him, to see what comes after.

The house will be cluttered, the carpet a mess
Our only recourse will be a change of address.
Leave the kids to their fun, I'll come up with a way
To get my work done before the big day.

With one day to go, it all seemed so tragic.
My office was dull and devoid of all magic.
My phone, it did ring, and I answered the call.

Wondering how in the world I would manage it all.

When a voice so familiar spoke in my ear
"How's it going?" Sis asked. "The big day is near."
Don't fear, I calmed her, the store has the bird.
They said they would thaw it. They gave me their word.

As I drove home that night, the bird in the trunk
I thought of the lonely, the hungry, the sunk.
Did I have it all wrong? Could I be so mistaken?
It's not about food, or when I'll awaken.

It's not about cleaning or even the baking.
It's how we give thanks for what we are taking.
I made up my mind to be the best host
Spending time with the ones that I love the most.

As we sat at the table, I took in the sight
Of my family around me and safe on that night.
After saying our grace, we counted each blessing
Then helped ourselves to spoonfuls of dressing.
Happy Thanksgiving to all and to all a good bite!

~ Christmas Curmudgeon ~

With every moment of our waking hours typically scheduled to the "nth" degree, plate spinners, by definition, have little tolerance for activities that are seemingly without purpose. As such, I hope you'll indulge my scrutiny of one such time-draining Christmas tradition—standing in line to see Santa.

While decorating the tree, sending cards, and baking cookies, in comparison, are worthwhile pursuits because you have something to show for your time and effort, I'd like to argue that prowling parking lots in inclement weather to get a space within a mile of a busy shopping center just so I can queue up to snap a shot of my child sitting on Santa's lap, holds little merit.

I speak from experience.

When our oldest was a year and a half and his little brother was just two months old, we were persuaded to take part in this ritual by my husband's best friend who had landed a gig as one of the Santas down at Marshall Field's on State Street. So, on an unseasonably bitter Saturday in December, we packed up the buggy and the boys and made our way downtown. Thankfully, as was their way, that grand old store pulled out all the stops to get everyone in the holiday spirit.

We cheerfully plodded forward, becoming mesmerized by all of the twinkling displays and the delightful holiday music—so much so that we were oblivious to the fact that we were about to plop a little boy and a baby, both of whom had very ripe diapers, into Santa's lap. The boys didn't care, but we were mortified, especially when we learned that my husband's friend's shift had ended fifteen minutes earlier.

When I was little, we didn't go to the store to see Santa. He came to us, riding down our street in a station wagon that looked suspiciously like ours with an old red police light affixed to the dashboard. On Christmas Eve, right after dinner, my sister and I huddled excitedly on the curb with our best friends from across the street. Even with snow whirling around us in the dark, we could see him coming down the block.

We'd leap up, shrieking our greetings. When they slowly passed by, we'd see the big guy, looking suspiciously like our friends' Dad, sitting on the tailgate, laughing and tossing candy out to us. I can still hear the snow crunch under the weight of the car's chain-wrapped tires as we scurried after it looking for candy canes and chocolate coins.

No, I didn't actually sit on his lap and recite my wish list, but I figured that if he saw that I wasn't knocking my sister over trying to get the most candy, I'd still land a spot on his "nice" list. My Mom, in the meantime, got to relax in the warmth of our kitchen, enjoying coffee with the rest of the mothers on our block.

At least, I think it was coffee.

~ Contemplate Christmas Greetings ~

Maybe it's the flurry of leaves blowing from the tree in my backyard. Perhaps it's the premature appearance of peppermint ice cream in the grocery store's freezer section. Or it could be because the stores are already phasing out all things creepy and replacing them with all things yuletide-y. Personally, I think it's because radio stations are poised to play Christmas carols 24/7 just hours after we finish trick-or-treating.

Whatever the case, the proactive plate spinner in me is ready to pull out my candy cane pen and draft our first annual family Christmas letter. For the past eighteen years, I've gotten by with the standard photo card. Granted, the more boys we've added, getting that group shot has become more of a challenge. I can only hope the recipients have appreciated the measure to which I have gone to get one with them all smiling in it—even if it is through gritted teeth.

But, this year will be different.

Since I'm relatively new to this exercise, all I have to fall back on are memories of my busy Mom tackling the task just a week or two before the big day. She'd station herself at the head of the kitchen table, typewriter at the ready, her overstuffed address book on one side and a box of cards on the other. I remember my Dad getting a nifty little plastic postage stamp dispenser, along with an address stamp and an ink pad so, when Mom was ready, my siblings and I could form an assembly line to help her fold, stuff, address, and stamp the cards. Just like Santa's elves. Despite the stress my harried working Mom must've felt at the time, we looked forward to this family tradition as much as putting up the tree.

I don't recall ever reading any of the letters she typed, but I'm sure they contained the same glowing accounts of our accomplishments as the ones we'd receive from relatives and friends. They'd always start with a phrase like, "Greetings from (insert name of tropical locale) where we vacationed this summer!" Or, "Hey-Ho, Neighbors—Yule never believe what's been happening with the (insert last name of over achievers down the street)!"

The letters would then go on to regale us with stories about how their child landed a spot on Bozo's Circus or was one of the first in line at the brand new Disney amusement park in Orlando, Florida.

Ho, ho, ho...

Staring at the blank screen on my laptop, writer's block settles over me like a foot of wet snow. Let's see. We weren't able to squeeze in a family vacation this year. Not unless you include the time we managed to get all five kids in the car to go see a movie. Sweat starts to bead on my forehead and I discover my candy can pen doesn't taste like peppermint at all.

I type, "Greetings from suburbia where we survived the year!" and call it a day.

~ A Holiday Survival Guide ~

When I sink into the couch after shelving the last of the Thanksgiving dinner dishes, the last thing I want to see is my husband thumbing through the "Black Friday" ads or my sons pulling out the Christmas decorations. Having added Thanksgiving prep to my usual plate-spinning routine for the past couple of weeks now, I know I need a breather, a break between the major holidays. But, like my time-starved mother before me, I know that taking a reprieve is a luxury I just cannot afford.

So, how can working parents successfully downshift from the season of gorging to the season of giving? For me, it's simple—eat, pray, crochet.

Proper nutrition is key. While the caffeine-and-refined-sugar diet has seen me through many a holiday season, this may not work for everyone. Counting calories, however, is an easy way to prevent a waistline expansion that will have you pining for a health club membership a month from now. If you choose wisely, there's no need to feel deprived. For instance, six ounces of eggnog is 300 calories. So is an eight-ounce hunk of broiled, skinless chicken breast. You decide.

And remember, slogging through crowded store aisles with children in tow does hold some calorie-burning potential, especially when pushing a stroller and lugging large packages.

Feeding your soul is equally important. Again, it's all about choices. Some people pray that they make it to the store in time to get that must-have item on their Christmas shopping list. Others pray that they receive that must-have item on their list. The wise ones, though, have figured out that the only way to fill their soul is to meet the needs of others.

Check it out. The next time you barrel into the grocery store, instead of passing the guy ringing a bell, drop some cash in his bucket. Or, on your way to work, instead of ignoring that guy sitting on the street with his head down while he's holding out a battered cup, drop some change in it or, better yet, hand him a sandwich. You may just find that having that latest flashing gadget isn't so important after all.

Last, but not least, crochet. It's my hobby of choice. Like my two-needled knitting counterparts, when stressed, I crave the mind-calming, thought-gathering charm that can only be found in the familiar rhythm of knotting yarn into something soft, beautiful, and useful. That's a double-bonus for this plate-spinning multitasker. On a Christmas morning that capped the most trying time of my career, I handed out enough handmade scarves and afghans to make Santa himself blush.

While I'm cognizant of the fact that not all working parents crochet or knit, I do recommend that you indulge in a hobby of your liking—photography or restoring classic cars. If it results in a potential gift, all the better.

Now, if you'll excuse me, I have a thousand things to do...

~ *The Power of Peppermint* ~

Any plate spinner worth their weight in peppermint bark will tell you that it's all about maintaining balance—a constant challenge, especially during the holidays. Such is the case in my house.

As sure as candy canes have stripes, I know that my children's level of excitement over the upcoming holidays will peak on the last day of school before winter break. Conversely, I know that the slow crescendo of holiday-prep stress that I'm trying to fend off will likely peak on their first official day home on winter break.

For them, the countdown to Christmas is measured by daily doses of chocolate plundered from their Advent calendars. For me, it's measured by activities that I am not able to tick off of my to-do list. Ho, ho, hum. And, as they look forward to weeks of unscheduled, unencumbered free time, I am starting to feel the balance between work and family life get a little off kilter. Holiday stuff—things like stuffing stockings, wrapping gifts, and decking the halls, are being pushed to the back burner.

With one camp focused on leisure and the other focused on labor, I fear a veritable train wreck is imminent. I'm picturing restless children scouring the house, not to clean it, but to find presents. Or perhaps, they'll devour the packaged cookies I bought for the big guy in the red suit and I'll have to make more. From scratch. Worse yet, what if they simply spend the entire time watching TV, playing video games and, well, taking a break on their break?

We will somehow have to reach a compromise between my need to be activity-bound and their desire to be unbound. Granted, the give and take required from both sides poses its own challenges.

For instance, state driving laws notwithstanding, I know that sending my driver-permitted, but unlicensed son to the mall to get last-minute gifts is just not an option. On the other hand, squeezing a few additional minutes out of my day to focus on having fun would be a possibility, I suppose, if we lived in a world where things like daily showers and sleep were not essential for maintaining a moderate level of civility.

So much for compromise.

I begin to wonder if praying for a blizzard might hold some merit. What with all of the shoveling, sledding, snowball fights, snowman building, and snow angel-making, several inches of snow would keep them occupied for hours, if not days. A native of Chicago's suburbs, I know the odds are in my favor for a white Christmas. With so much still to do, though, I grapple for a back-up plan.

About to draft a lengthy to-do list to keep my boys otherwise occupied during their break, I reach for my trusty candy cane pen, sticking the end in my mouth as I contemplate what still needs to be done. The burst of peppermint takes me by surprise. Clearly someone had swapped my pen for the real thing. Hearing giggles come from the other room, I get up to confront the culprits and thank them for restoring my holiday spirit.

~ *You Had Me at "Ho!"* ~

Dear Santa,

Since my kids are drafting their letters to you, I thought I'd take this opportunity to drop you a line.

Don't worry. This isn't another self-promoting letter intended to garner lots of presents in exchange for good behavior. I just want you to know that, as the manager of a to-do list that would make a grown plate spinner cry, you're nothing short of a multitasking super hero.

I'm a huge fan.

Granted, like any other big celebrity, you have a support staff, albeit height-challenged and pointy-eared, but still—I am humbled by your ability to travel the globe, shimmying into all sorts of domiciles to deliver packages in the course of one fleeting night.

I can't imagine the miles you must have racked up on that sleigh of yours over the years. In comparison, how can I complain about having to race back to one of my boys' schools in my tired old Buick just to deliver a forgotten lunch or buzz to the grocery store twice in one day to replenish my pantry?

Still, I suppose it helps that you only deliver to the folks on your "nice" list. Personally, I have found the whole concept of children having to secure a spot on this coveted list a highly valuable parenting tool. So, thanks for that.

I'd like to commend you on your outfit as well. I've never had my colors done, but red definitely works for you. It brings out the glow in your cheeks and adds to the sparkle in your eyes. And, as an alumnus of the parochial school system, I can certainly appreciate the time savings inherent in wearing a uniform.

As to the multitude of men who try to emulate you, just remember—imitation is the highest form of flattery.

Some may bear an uncanny resemblance, but nothing foils a fake Santa faster than a crying baby.

Nonetheless, despite my best efforts, I want you to know that I couldn't pull off this holiday without you. I may trim the tree, mail the cards, troll shopping center parking lots, make all manner of Christmas cookies, and put little foil-wrapped chocolate versions of you in my kids' stockings, but you're the one that brings a certain magical stress-free excitement to the season—no matter how old I get.

I just need to work on the stress-free part. By the time Christmas eve rolls around, I check where you are on the NORAD website, then rather gruffly order my kids to bed, warning them that you won't stop by unless they're sleeping.

How you maintain that jolly disposition, I'll never know. I suppose that megadose of sugar you ingest during your travels helps. Whatever the reason, you're truly an inspiration. It's a wonder working parents aren't lining up in droves for a chance to sit on your lap in shopping malls across the country, asking for your autograph.

But enough gushing.

The bottom line is, you complete me. Just don't tell Mrs. Claus, ok? I wouldn't want to make the "naughty" list.

Signed,
The Plate Spinner

~ *A Cautionary Carol* ~

My Mom is no ghost, but as Christmas approaches, the sheer volume of homemade cookies and gifts that she used to produce when she was in her plate-spinning prime haunts me. Even Martha Stewart couldn't hold her spatula.

All this while working full-time and raising five kids—without a microwave. Those are some mighty big pumps to fill.

With a few minutes to spare between one son's piano lesson and another son's dental appointment, I popped in recently for a quick visit. A familiar scent greeted me at the door. Turns out, she was spending the day making her traditional, labor-intensive date nut bread. It wouldn't be Christmas without it.

Guilt started wrapping around me like a heavy chain. I didn't dare tell her about how I came this close to leaving out store-bought cookies for Santa the year before.

Instead, I announced that one of my boys signed me up to make treats for a class party the next day.

"Like I don't have enough to do," I fumed.

She noted my stress. "You'd better slow down or you're going to miss it."

"Miss what?" I mumbled, shoving a hunk of the warm bread in my mouth.

"Christmas."

I smirked at her. "You say that like it's a bad thing. I'm actually looking forward to it being over."

I ignored her gasp, grabbed the date nut bread she had set aside for me, kissed her good-bye and headed out the door.

That night, I was visited by three bad dreams. Either that, or I was paying the price for not sharing that loaf of date nut bread with my kids.

In the first dream, I watched as a much younger version of myself sat in my mom's lap in a chair in our living room. Christmas carols were coming out of our hi-fi and we were both admiring the twinkling lights on the tree. I marveled at the peaceful stillness. No hustle. No bustle. Just enjoying the moment.

From there, I was whisked into a troubling scene. I saw myself burst into our kitchen after a long day at the office and brusquely explain to my sweet-natured, hopeful son why we absolutely could not make the brownies he was hoping to bring to his class party because I was too tired and still had so many things to do before I could go to bed.

My heart broke as I took in the expression on his face. How could I be so selfish?

But it got better. When my older son joined us and offered to make the brownies for me while I relaxed, I turned on him. I grabbed the box, cranked on the oven, pulled out a mixing bowl, and ordered them both out of the kitchen.

That's when the real nightmare started. The lights in the kitchen went out and I was utterly alone. Not the kind of alone I typically long for. The kind of alone that there's no coming back from.

I woke up with a start. The house was still quiet and dark, but far from empty. Relieved, I headed downstairs to bake some brownies.

God bless us, every one!

~ *Rushing to Resolutions* ~

'Tis the season to be rushing. There are gifts to deliver, parties to attend, and treats to make all by a very particular day. Since working parents by nature rush to and through everything—meetings, appointments, errands, conversations, and meals—we are in our element. Try as we might, even when all those around us have the presence of mind to be in the moment, we can't help but to race on to the next thing that has to be done, said, or planned.

Holidays are no exception. Take Christmas. Tradition practically mandates that all of this holiday's plates be spun and shelved the night before. The gifts must be purchased, wrapped, and strategically placed under the recipient's tree, the cookies baked and set out for the big guy, and the plans for the feast set. Technically, the only plate spinning that should be going on is remembering to set your coffeemaker to "auto" before you go to bed and deciding whether you'd like a sprinkle of nutmeg on your eggnog.

And yet, barely an hour into our Christmas day celebration, I'll grab a recently-crumpled piece of wrapping paper off of my living room floor, retrieve a candy cane pen from my stocking, help myself to a hefty piece of homemade coffee cake, and begin drafting a list of New Year's resolutions.

An annual rite of self-improvement, resolutions are akin to a home-based, personal performance review. At work, I'm assessed against how well I have met the objectives I penned for the previous year. At home, I assess myself. Topping my list since I was fourteen is "eat less, exercise more."

I pause to enjoy another bite of coffeecake.

Since the program manager in me demands measurable results, I try to recall the specifics. Did I meet the frequency and target goals I had set for myself? Staring at the lights on our tree, my eyes glaze over as I push these resolutions aside and consider replacing them with items of a more philanthropic nature such as volunteering at my kids' schools or maybe the local food bank.

"Mom, can you read this to me?" The spell is broken.

"What?" I ask as my first grader climbs into my lap.

Holding up a new book, he again asks if I will read to him. A knee-jerk reaction prompts me to reply, "How about you read it to me while I—"

Casting his big browns on me, his lower lip protruding just a touch, he waits for me to finish.

Defenseless against such a brazen assault on my sensibilities, I ball up my list, cap my pen, and say, "Wait. I have a great idea. How about you finish my coffee cake while I read this book to you?"

Smiling, he snuggles close and polishes off my breakfast while I take a moment to be in the moment.

~ Should Auld Acquaintance Be Forgot ~

Somewhere between the last strains of "White Christmas" and the beginning chords of "Auld Lang Syne," plate spinners begin contemplating plans for the upcoming year. We can't help it. It's what we do. Brand new calendars seduce us with blank pages just waiting to be filled in. We excitedly rub our hands together, setting our sights on the vast, clean expanse that beckons every January 1st. So many plans to put into motion and resolutions to kick start.
Just keep spinning, just keep spinning.
Before you know it, like a gerbil on its exercise wheel, we're on the road to the "crazy" store—that place my mom always said she was going when I asked her where she was headed.
So this year, before zooming onto this road to nowhere, I am going to force myself to stop, turn around, and look back on this past year. Taking the time to reflect on my accomplishments and consider any mistakes I may have made is not only rejuvenating, it helps me adjust my goals and right my wrongs before strapping myself in for another plate-spinning ride.
My dearest friend taught me this nifty lesson when we were roommates in college. At the end of each semester, I would impulsively look forward, fretting over things like which classes to take next, whether I should stay on campus for the summer, and if she thought I was nuts to dare that guy I had just met to go out with me. Pretty heavy stuff. Nonetheless, with her last final behind her, my BFF, a graduate student majoring in counseling, seized the opportunity to practice her newly learned skills.
At the pizza place that was not only our place of employment but our second home when we lived off campus, she would sit me down and conduct a retrospective on the prior term. Pointing out my accomplishments—

everything from teaching idioms to a class of Vietnamese students as part of my graduate assistantship to mastering the fine art of rolling pizza dough, she reminded me of how far I had come since the beginning of the year. She'd also remind me of the hard, albeit not earth-shattering, decisions I had to make during that time, like whether to spend a portion of my student loan money on a bus pass so I could get to my internship or on a new perm.

All in all, a pizza and a pitcher later, all was right with the world and I knew exactly what I had to do. Even to this day, she is there for me. Living an hour apart, we occasionally catch up over lunch, assuring each other and laughing at our missteps. We can't help it. It's what we do.

Oh, and that guy I dared to ask me out? That would be my husband of over twenty years.

CHAPTER EIGHT

It's Better to Look Good Than to Spin Good

~ Ghosts of Haircuts Past ~

When I got laid off from my job several years back, the first expense to get exorcised from my budget was hair care. No more going in for trims every six to eight weeks, spending a small fortune on products and procedures intended to force my hair into something nature was simply never intending.

After years of sporting a multilayer, permed, and highlighted "do," I allowed my fine, pin-straight hair to grow into the long and silky style reminiscent of my seventh grade class picture. And, for this plate spinner—forever short on time, vanity, and cash—the style worked. Its versatility was a boon. I could pull it back into a clip, swoop it up into a ponytail, clump it into a bobby-pinned knot or, for an ultra-sleek look, do absolutely nothing to it except tuck it behind my ears.

Aside from daily washings and the occasional conditioning, for the next couple of years, I ignored my hair and pleas from my stylishly coiffed sister, begging me to, at the very least, go in for a trim. In a charitable mood, I concurred and let a stylist lop off several inches that I promptly donated. It grew back in no time.

Then it happened.

Last December, at our high school band's Christmas concert, we perused the silent auction items. In hindsight, I did find my sister's feverish bidding for a free haircut at a local salon a bit odd. When she let out a victory yell that could drown out a 747, I understood what she was going to do with her prize.

"Here." She handed me the ribboned salon brochure. I looked down at it.

Good for one free haircut with Alissa was written in flowery pink cursive. All that was missing was a little heart over the "i."

A knot formed in my stomach.

Six months later, I dialed the number. The perky voice on the other end suggested a time a few days out. I gulped and said, "That would be fine."

Brochure in hand, I made my way to the salon. Before long, I was in Alissa's chair letting her weave her fingers through my hair as she examined it, asking, "So…what are we going to do today?"

I fought back the urge to say, "I'm looking for a style that will require me to come in for frequent trims and use several products and appliances so I can spend at least an hour styling it each morning and not have a prayer of getting it to look as good as it will when I walk out of here."

Instead, I blurted out, "Whatever you think, as long as it's easy to take care of, flatters my features, and does not make me look like every other working mother in this county."

An hour later, I walked out with a haircut reminiscent of my third grade picture—a blunt, shoulder-length cut with bangs.

At least it will be easy to grow out…

~ *Quick Change Artist* ~

At my office, most employees' desks are covered with framed photos, knick-knacks, plants, and candy dishes. Not mine. The sleek line of my faux-granite-top desk is obstructed by just a few neat stacks of notes and a desktop organizer stuffed with pens and paperclips.
While my coworkers may debate the virtues of an uncluttered desk, they agree that multitasking is a vital workplace skill. What they don't realize is that my daytime job is a walk in the park compared to the real plate spinning that goes on when I walk out the door at the end of the day.
At work, I excel. I'm responsible for my own success or failure. Never mind the smudge of oatmeal on my shoulder (remnants of a good-bye hug). Never mind the run in my pantyhose (not noticed until sitting next to my manager in a status meeting). Bring on the frantic sales people, the frustrated customers. Push up my deadlines and come to me with complaints. Ah! Another phone call. Bring it on.
"Good morning!" (pause) "Uh, no I don't know where your library books are." I lower my voice. "Put Dad on the phone." (silence, followed by loud bang of receiver being dropped on a wooden chair in our kitchen, then a shrill "Dad! Mom wants to talk to you!")
I hold the phone away from my head to prevent my eardrum from rupturing. Heads in my work area begin to turn. My husband gets on the line with an exasperated, "Yeah?"
I hear his plates crashing in the background. This morning was to be the premiere of his amazing "Drop the Boys Off to Day Care and Elementary School At the Same Time When The Schools Are Two Miles Apart" routine.
I crouch over my phone, "Everything OK?"
"Oh, just the usual. Trying to get out the door."

I hang up, take a deep breath, and remind myself that long-distance plate spinning is not in my job description. I check my schedule and prepare for my next meeting.

When the workday is behind me, I open the front door to our house. My husband is waiting for me in the foyer and, like an airport runway traffic manager—without the big headphones and orange glow sticks—he silently waves me up the stairs before the kids notice I'm home. In the quiet of our bedroom, I shed my work costume and put on my at-home ensemble of jeans and a sweater.

I rejoin my husband who in turn announces, "Mom's home!"

All five boys rush in simultaneously telling me about their day. "Can you help me with a paper?"

My husband tosses me a plate. "I need help with my math homework!"

I toss a plate to my husband. "What's for supper?"

I reach my hand up and grab another plate.

"Mom, how come you didn't come to our concert this morning?"

Blindsided, I hear a plate crash to the floor.

With that, my husband clears the crowd, pulls me close and asks, "So, how was work today?"

I sigh and tell him, "Oh, my work is just beginning."

~ Raiders of the Clothes Closet ~

With five busy boys, a full-time job, and aspirations of literary grandeur, I have little time or tolerance for clothes shopping. In fact, if given the choice, I'd rather be strapped to a chair and forced to watch reality TV. There. I said it.

Truth be told, I have never had the ability or desire to keep up with current trends. But with two older sisters, I never really had to. Inheriting hand-me-downs became my only means to a well-dressed end. It didn't matter how old the clothes were. Being the youngest meant that wearing something my older siblings, or even my Mom, at one time possessed was the coolest thing ever.

Or so they told me.

Waiting to take possession, though, was the hardest part. The twelve years I spent in parochial school only compounded the problem. Wearing the same uniform day after day, the only fashion muscle I got to flex was deciding whether I should wear a long- or short-sleeve blouse.

By the time I was finally old enough to go to dances, I had become a closet-raiding fashionista. Into their closets I would plunge, trying on all of the wrap skirts, gauchos, and cowl-neck sweaters I could get my hands on. Anything, as long as it wasn't made of plaid wool.

Salvation came when I started college. The designer-clothes bug that ravaged large sectors of the population in the early Eighties bit my mom hard. Her symptoms included prowling the high-end fashion mall on her lunch hour and accumulating all of the Liz Claiborne, Evan Picone, and Ralph Lauren blouses, skirts, and shoes that she could carry.

Although her affliction was highly contagious, I was living on campus at the time. As a result, my bout with the bug was relatively mild. While I didn't feel the urge to actually purchase designer clothes, I did feel compelled to raid her closet while home on breaks. Thankfully, the designer duds I permanently borrowed saw me through graduation, my first job interviews, and the next few years that followed until I was faced with the biggest fashion challenge yet—what to wear on my wedding day.

Determined to self-finance the affair, my fiancé and I had agreed on a budget. With an image of Princess Di's dress, a vision of pearl beading and ivory taffeta, swirling in my head, I dragged my bridesmaids along on my quest for the THE dress—the one that would make me look like royalty, but not go over my limit.

After plowing through a dozen stores, I came to the sad conclusion that it didn't exist.

That's when my Mom invited me to raid her closet again. Turns out, THE dress was there the entire time. All it needed was a talented seamstress who magically, and quite economically, refurbished the beautiful circa 1952 Cinderella ball gown into a vision of Chantilly lace and tulle.

And on the big day, I felt like the coolest bride ever.

~ Fitting in Fitness ~

It started innocently enough. Rushing to get dressed in the dark of a recent morning, I grabbed a clean pair of jeans out of the laundry basket, eyeballed the length, and pulled them on. Twenty minutes later, I was pouring a cup of coffee in the kitchen absently wondering why the pants I had on felt, well, a little funny.

Then it happened.

"Mom. Are you wearing my jeans?"

He may as well have told me that I had a spider crawling on me.

"What? Of course not!" I gasped as I quickly examined my legs wondering how the denim covering them had gotten so torn and worn looking.

I blame the long winter that kept me inside baking cookies and casseroles and away from my walking routine. Nonetheless, it was an unsolicited pre-pool-season wake up call.

While my weight still falls within a normal range for my height, things are starting to shift south. I know this shouldn't surprise me. I'm finding out the hard way that age and gravity are BFFs. Combine that with the fact that working parents are notorious for putting the needs of others before their own, and I am not sure what to do about my, um, predicament.

Like it or not, the whole "eat-less-exercise-more-reduce-stress" mantra flies in the face of the plate-spinning lifestyle. We eat fast food on the go and guzzle coffee like a semi does diesel. Even through all five pregnancies, I credited my caffeine-and-refined-sugar diet for keeping me alert in staff meetings and well within the weight limits dictated by my mortified obstetrician.

My sister, well versed in all things weight loss, recommended cutting back on sugar. After I stopped laughing, I argued the futility of her plan. High fructose corn syrup is hidden in everything from breakfast cereal to shampoo. There's no getting around it, even if I wanted to.

As for exercise, I attribute my bicep of steel (right arm only) to the coffee curl reps I make a point of getting in each morning. More weight training, really. What I need is regular aerobic exercise. And to stick with something like that, I need a motivating element. Something with a deadline.

My son, a runner and, yes, the true owner of the jeans I had mistakenly swiped, waved a recently-received postcard at me. It announced reduced early entry fees for a 5k race scheduled for early June. "I dare you," he said, handing it to me with a smirk.

Not one to back down from a challenge, I snatched the postcard and examined the fine print closely. The words "free T-shirts to the first 2000 registered runners" popped out at me.

I returned his smirk.
Bring it.
Now, pass the pasta. I'm in training!

~ The Ultimate Spring Cleaning Workout ~

Is house cleaning something you keep shoving to the greasy back burner because there's always something more important to do?

Do you long for the promise of increased energy and stamina that comes with regular exercise, but just can't seem to find the time?

Let me introduce you to "The Plate Spinner's Ultimate Spring Cleaning Workout"!

This simple plan has the combined effect of leaving you with a house that sparkles, enough energy to leave a certain drum-beating fuzz ball in your tracks, and, best of all, a shorter to-do list. Only a true plate-spinning superhero could appreciate that kind of efficiency.

First, warm-up.

Start by locating a shelf in your house that needs decluttering. For this example, let's use a bedroom closet. Be sure to have a box labeled "Goodwill" (or the charity of your choice) at the ready.

Stand directly in front of the shelf. Using a step stool or chair, reach your arms up to grasp an item worthy of donation (e.g., an old Smith-Corona in need of a nonexistent repairman, an old photo album filled with Pokemon cards, or a box containing a hot pot that was last used when Michael Jackson first moon-walked across the TV screen).

Slowly lift the object off of the shelf and hold until you feel the muscles in your arms and back start to throb.

Replace the object to its original spot when you think you hear your spouse or child approaching. Repeat twice and place the item in the box.

Next, cardio. You have a couple of options here—pushing a vacuum, waxing your car, or scrubbing the kitchen floor.

For this example, I'll choose the latter because it has the added bonus of getting a facial when you hold your face over a bucket of steaming water.

Remove all moveable objects from your kitchen—chairs, table, children, etc. Remember to lift with your legs!

Get two buckets. Fill one with water and a soap that is strong enough to get petrified egg yolk and permanent marker off of your linoleum. Fill the other bucket with steaming hot water for rinsing.

Snap on some rubber gloves and pull out a scrub brush and big fat sponge. I recommend sliding a butter knife in your back pocket to have handy should you come across a lump of dried gum or some unidentifiable caked-on gook.

Starting in the corner farthest from the doorway, dunk the scrub brush in the soapy water and vigorously work it over the floor. When you feel the muscles in one arm take on the consistency of Jell-O, switch hands, but don't forget—constant movement is key.

As you rinse the soap off of the floor, remember to hold your face over the bucket to open and cleanse your pores.

When the entire floor is done, dash to the nearest mirror so you can admire your healthy glow.

Lastly, cool down. I recommend a leisurely activity like, say, dusting.

Find a soft cloth (old cloth diapers or swatches of fabric cut from old bridesmaid dresses are ideal).

Run it across any dusty surface—coffee tables, ceiling fan blades, half-finished craft projects, or the box of VHS tapes, the majority of which contain every highlight of your oldest child's young life and about 10 minutes worth of your youngest's.

Congratulations!

Your house is now cleaner, your waistline is trimmer, and your to-do list is shorter, but best of all—you'll look stunning when you pull up to Goodwill.

CHAPTER NINE

You Are What You Spin

~ A Largely Relative Question ~

Dear Plate Spinner,
I noticed you label your family as "relatively large." I have friends who have anywhere from one to seven children and I am acquainted with a family of nine children. What does our culture consider a "large" family?
Jennifer (mother of five and one on the way)

Dear Jennifer,
Thank you for your question! With five children, I used the qualifier "relatively" because I am well aware that, compared to the size of some families, five children may seem like a drop in the bucket, while, for other families, the thought of having five children may send them into a fit of delirious laughter.
I don't know what our culture considers to be a "large" family, but if you experience any of the following, it's pretty much a no-brainer:
— When people learn of the size of your family, they typically exclaim "My, you must have your hands full!" or "There's a special place for you in heaven!"
— When you try to book a hotel room for a family vacation, the person taking your call suggests that you reserve a block of rooms.

— When shopping for a vehicle that will fit your entire family, you find yourself at a shuttle bus dealership.

— When grocery shopping for the week, you can usually be found pushing one cart down the aisle while pulling another behind you.

— When one of your younger children comes home from school complaining that the teacher called him by every older sibling's name before getting to theirs.

— When making a recipe that is supposed to serve four, you double or even triple the ingredients.

— When your grocery bill is the largest expense on your monthly budget.

— When attending a religious service, your family takes up an entire pew.

— When you find yourself changing out dishwashers and laundry machines as often as the oil in your car.

There may not be a cultural norm when it comes to family size, but no matter what the size of your family, certain plates must still be spun—meal planning and prep, house cleaning, child-rearing, career tending, homework monitoring, and financial management, just to name a few.

Members of large families can extol the virtues and drawbacks of their size just as members of smaller families can. What I do know is that the size of my family is just right for us.

Now, if I could just get Rob, argh, Russ, uh, Dan, geez, Chris, ugh, I mean James, to make his bed, I'd be happy.

~ Meal Planning ~

Well-documented research suggests that if families would simply sit down to have dinner together each night, a maelstrom of social, economic, and environmental ailments would be eliminated—everything from teenage angst to global warming. Is it the nutritious meals or maybe the stimulating conversation?

Whatever the reason, the merit of sit-down dinners was certainly not lost on my parents. I have fond memories of eating with them and my older sisters and brothers. Every single night.

Now I've heard of people who can survey the scant contents of their pantry shelves and miraculously whip together near-gourmet concoctions much to the delight and amazement of their family and friends. I'm not one of them.

In those pre-microwave days, my mom, in the few frenzied moments she had between arriving home from work and my dad walking through the door expecting a hot meal, was somehow able to whip together a meat and potato combo hearty enough to satisfy his 6'5" appetite. Little was said at these meals. I learned early on not to make eye contact with my older sister who, at every opportunity, made the goofiest expression on her face to try and get me to laugh. The first time she did this to her naive little sister, I laughed so hard I spilled my milk and fell backward in my chair. Some fun.

So, what's caused this cherished family event to land a spot on the endangered species list? Is it our constant lack of time? Maybe. But, with the advent of microwave cooking, time is no longer an essential element in putting three square meals on the table. Let's face it. We don't want speed. We just want more time. There's a difference.

In my house, our schedules are not the only thing straining at full capacity. We have one woefully small refrigerator. It harkens back to the days when we were a four-person family. It can hold a gallon of milk, a carton of juice, a dozen eggs, a pound of butter, and a loaf of bread. In the produce drawer, I can squeeze an apple and one or two pearl onions. The freezer can hold a box of fish sticks, one mini ice cube tray, and a twin-pop. Nonetheless, it still works like a charm and we are loath to part with it. But, I digress.

This simple four-step plan can help transform you from a harried working parent who crawls through the door after a long commute with just enough energy to curl up in the corner with a cookbook in one hand and the pizza delivery guy's number in the other to a meal-planning, plate-spinning pro:

1. Identify easy-to-make meals that do not require:
   a. ingredients you cannot pronounce without having taken four semesters of conversational French in college, and
   b. more than 15 minutes of prep time (not including shopping).

2. List all of the ingredients you need to make meals for the next two days (or more if your fridge has a capacity of at least 24 cubic ft.)
   a. Make sure you don't already have these items before you list them. The average spice rack does not need more than one container of coriander.
   b. Scan the grocery store ads to see where you can get the ingredients for the best possible price (especially important if you're saving up for a larger refrigerator). Match the items pictured in the ads against the items on your list, like a culinary game of mahjong.
3. Determine how far in advance you can make each meal. Some food items, once prepared, can survive a day or two

in your freezer very nicely. (Note: Tuna salad is not one of them. Trust me.)

And, for what it's worth, my fondest family mealtime memories all stem from the nights when my Dad would burst through the door, stressed after a long hard day, see how tired and equally frazzled my Mom was, and tell everybody, "Get in the car! We're going to Hamburger Heaven!"

On the drive home, in the cavernous back seat of the family sedan, I would relish the last of my root beer float, knowing full well that it beat having to sit silently at a tense dinner table trying to not make eye contact with my sister who was determined to show me her latest rendition of "see-food."

~ The Grocery Getaway ~

Yes, I've heard of people who can survey the scant contents of their pantry shelves and miraculously whip together near-gourmet concoctions much to the delight and amazement of their family and friends. I'm not one of them.

One of my heaviest, not to mention slippery, plates to spin is grocery shopping because it spins perilously close to my meal-planning and coupon-clipping plates, the latter of which I often let fall.

With five boys whose appetites range between a ravenous "there's-nothing-to-eat" teenager and a finicky "I-only-want-popcorn" preschooler, I know the cashiers at my local grocery store better than some of my extended family members.

My husband is the coupon clipper and sales scout, but I am the list maker. While it's not often that my list actually reflects what he's scouted and clipped, I proceed with my plan undeterred.

Often, I'll bring at least one of my five boys for some quality time with Mom so we can talk without interruption on the drive to the store. This is how the conversation typically goes:

Me: "So, how's it going?"
Son: "Fine."

All is right with the world.

Deciding which son to bring is simple. When they see me head for the front door, coupon clutch securely in the crux of my elbow and car keys in hand, they pop up from their seats in the living room like so many prairie dogs popping up through the grass on a hot summer day.

"Where ya goin'?" they ask in unison, their gaze never leaving the TV.

"Crazy," I matter-of-factly reply, just to see if I'll get the usual "Oh, can I come?" from any of them in reply.

The one who has managed to peel his eyes from the TV is chosen as a reward for their über-sharp listening skills.

Any one of my older three boys is preferred to their younger siblings. They can go fetch things that I forget without me having to leave the line. They can go to the bathroom by themselves if nature calls during the midst of a harried tour of the produce department that leaves me wondering since when did the definition of "fresh" include words like "bruised" and "mashed." They truly earn the quarter I dig out of my pocket for a quick spin at the gumball machine.

Not so with my younger two. They bring their own special joys to the grocery shopping experience—namely, grabbing things not on my list off the shelves, opening cereal boxes before they are purchased just to find the prize, and charming the deli counter lady out of a free piece of cheese. All this from one of those innocuous, cumbersome plastic nightmares that are supposed to seamlessly integrate the adult shopping experience with a child's sense of play and parental modeling. The car cart.

But my favorite time at the store is when the crowds have long gone and the boys are home in bed. Free to concentrate on my list, I rifle through the neatly categorized coupons filed in our kitschy clutch. As I peruse the aisles, I often find myself entering a Zen-like state, honing in on the targeted items, freely associating them with their place in the weekly menu, smirking at my inventiveness, all the while singing along to the old adult contemporary hits inevitably warbling from the store's speaker system.

The stock boys are used to seeing me blindly pushing my cart with my eyes glued to the shelves, singing perhaps a little too loudly to Taylor Dane's "Send Me a Lover" as if it were ladies night at the karaoke bar in aisle five.

~ Brown Bag Blues ~

Transitioning your family from a summer schedule to a decidedly hectic school schedule has the potential to make even the most seasoned plate spinners whimper in anticipation. While adapting to the rigors of jam-packed schedules can cause stress levels to spike, it only takes three simple words to send me over the edge—brown bag lunches.

When I was a kid, my siblings and I walked home for lunch where we'd dine on white bread, butter, cheese, and liver sausage sandwiches, prepared by our well-intentioned German grandmother. While I can feel my arteries harden at the memory, coming up with enticing and healthy options for my children's lunches is about as easy as lifting a pickup truck with a spoon.

Between the ever-confusing food pyramid, touting all things healthy, and the junk food infiltrating the media, hot lunch programs, and vending machines, our lunch bag menus have become, well, rather rigid.

My lunch prep plate has traditionally spun around a pantry stocked with fruit cups, snack bars, animal crackers, and not one, but two types of peanut butter—crunchy and smooth. In the fridge, there are always plenty of cheese sticks, baby carrots, and fresh fruit. Not especially trade-worthy, but a veritable cornucopia of nutrition. Yet, when consumed on a daily basis, they elicit yawns in each one of my boys.

Not averse to variety, I've occasionally peppered their options with bananas instead of jelly, graham crackers instead of animal crackers, and sliced cucumbers in place of carrots. But, still, they yawn. Pressured to come up with some real change, I waited for the opportune moment. The last day of school.

Food choices notwithstanding, our routine during the last school term worked like a well-oiled machine. Before the boys headed off to bed, we transformed our kitchen table into a lunch bag-stuffing, sandwich-making assembly line that would make even the busiest sandwich shops envious.

The older, taller boys would bring items down off the shelves while the younger ones laid out slices of bread and opened the peanut butter and jelly jars. At one end of the table sat the heavier objects—fruit usually—and, at the far end, open lunch bags into which they would deposit their choices. In between, they'd make their sandwiches and squeeze them into plastic baggies.

On the last night, when the glumness with which they normally faced this task was pleasantly outweighed by their euphoria over the approaching break, I casually asked them what they would like for lunch during the next year.

Despite the absence of confetti falling from the ceiling, you would've thought they had just won the lottery. Suggestions ranging from "anything but peanut butter" to "pepperoni slices" were volleyed back and forth, but none had the promise of peanut butter's easily stockable, buildable, and repeatable solution the plate-spinning project manager in me yearned for.

~ The Best Laid Plans ~

Last September, I surrendered to an irrepressible urge to get fit. That I announced my intention on my blog and tracked my progress there helped considerably. I ran my first-ever 5k in November.

Yet, as notable as this accomplishment was, it was not prominently featured on last year's resolutions. It didn't even make the top five. I checked.

Those resolutions that did top the list remain, for all intents and purposes, unfulfilled, and for very good reasons.

Case in point, resolution #2: Laugh a whole lot more. Foolishly, I didn't baseline my tendency to laugh, so I was unable to generate quantitative metrics for this one. Then there was #4: Be a positive role model for my kids—way too subjective. Finally, #5: Make a concerted effort to name your fears, stare them down, and conquer them. While I single-handedly conquered my fear of using the self-checkout lane at the grocery store, with coupons, my fear of heights remains a biggie. In this, I am learning to love myself for the chicken that I am.

So, as the New Year dawns, my list of resolutions is freakishly short. There is one thing, though, that must be included—sit down dinners with my family.

With our disparate schedules, mealtime in my kitchen resembles eating at a greasy spoon (minus the greasy spoon). Like a short-order cook, as soon as whatever quickie meal I've prepared is ready, I yell "Order up!" and start dishing out the grub to whoever is ready with a plate and an appetite.

As such, the same guilty conscience that prompted me to dust off and strap on my running shoes last fall, is now prompting me to gather the clan together each and every evening to enjoy a hot, nutritious meal.

Most working parents know this is so much easier said than done. There's the meal planning and cooking. Then, there's the battle against kitchen table clutter. Piles of school stuff, junk mail, newspapers, and magazines spring up on our kitchen table faster than dandelions in May.

But on this, I remain firm. Like the annual goals I have to submit to my manager each year, resolutions should be measurable and challenging enough to help me grow as a professional, but not entirely unattainable. Unlike the resolutions I set out to conquer last year, I think this one fits the bill.

It's certainly measurable. I can track how many nights we sit down to eat together. I can generate percentages and track trends. Heck, I can even generate a flashy, multi-colored chart, just for kicks. However, it has yet to be determined whether the challenge lies in the meal planning and prep or wrangling my gang to the table to eat together. And if this family dinnertime thing doesn't work out, there's always resolution #2: Train for a 10k.

~ Tales from the Pressure Cooker ~

No other time has as much impact on a person's life as the four years they spend in high school. And the pressure—to get good grades, make the team, fit in, stand out, blend in, and simply survive—will never be as intense.

I see my boys go through it every day. Hearing them talk, I'm transported back to my alma mater. I remember rushing through the halls, worried that I wouldn't make it to class in time and, if I did, I'd inevitably forget something I needed way back in my locker. The entire time, I'd avoid making eye contact with classmates who knew a dozen different ways to make me feel self-conscious.

Despite all of my rushing, time had an irritating way of feeling like it was standing completely still. On more than one occasion, it felt like high school would never end.

When I was in the thick of it, not happy with the way I looked, the clothes I wore, the minefield that was my complexion, and my pin-straight hair that, no matter how hard I tried, would never be as bouncy, curly, or cute as that of every popular girl in school, I would lament to my Mom.

Her first line of defense? She'd smile and tell me that things would get better.

That was a leap of faith I was never willing to make.

Next, she'd pull out the old standby "Just be yourself. The rest will follow." When that prompted me to wail even louder into my pillow, she'd dig deep and remind me of how proud she was of me no matter how I looked or how many friends I had. Eventually, that did the trick.

But even when I felt like all was right with my world, she never said, or led me to believe, that I was in the midst of the best years of my life. Maybe because she knew better. Or maybe because she wanted me to keep striving and growing into the person I was meant to be, learning to rise above any challenges I'd face not only then, but ever.

Man, she was good.

When I crossed the stage to accept my diploma, I felt the lid that had been on the pressure cooker of my life for the past four years blow clean off.

Whether you can't imagine life getting any better than it is right now or you can't wait to blaze your own trail on your terms, there is life after high school.

Like my Mom said, things will get better. You just have to keep the faith.

~ The Things We Do For Lent ~

When I was a kid, holidays were all about the candy. Halloween and candy corn, Christmas and candy canes, Valentine's Day and candy hearts. Now that I'm an adult, I tend to wonder whether the manufacturers of such confections are in league with the American Dental Association. It's hard enough to get my kids to see beyond the candy-coated exterior of any given holiday to understand its true meaning. But, all is not lost. With my busy schedule, early planning helps.

Luckily, most retailers are on board with this. The transition between holidays happens so quickly at some stores that, if you blink, you're likely to miss it. Take, for instance, Easter. As soon as the last sad boxes of rejected Valentine's Day cards are relegated to the discount bin, packages of neon-colored plastic eggs, baskets, and jelly beans take their place on the shelves.

In my house, things move at a snail's pace in comparison. Planning for Easter begins at the onset of Lent. Seated around the dinner table, I asked each child what they plan to give up for those forty days of preparation and deprivation. My youngest kicked off the discussion with one word.

"Broccoli."

Because of his tender age, I excused his naiveté and suggested that he do without something he really, really likes. I gently recommended chocolate milk, a staple in his diet.

Tender age notwithstanding, he sensed the hypocrisy in my suggestion, and countered with, "I will if you will."

I relented, bested by an eight year old. "Broccoli it is."

I moved on to one of my older boys. "Your turn. How about something electronic? How about Facebook?"

He winced. "Technically, Facebook isn't something electronic, is it?"

"Nice try."

Squirming, he reached into his pocket, pulled out his iPod and placed it on the table before me, careful not to make eye contact. Before I could say another word, the rest of the boys interrupted with their offerings.

"Chips."

"Soda."

"Gum."

My husband looked across the length of the table at me and asked, "And you?"

I admired his bravery.

Without hesitating, I smugly responded, "Coffee! Just like last year."

He held his head in his hands and mumbled, "Please, no. Not again."

I scoffed. "Well, what would you suggest?"

Again, perhaps because of the distance separating us from one end of the table to the other, he mustered the courage to suggest, "Chocolate."

Forty days is a very long time.

But, remembering that sacrifice is an integral part of this pre-Easter season, I agreed, determined to set an example for my boys.

I suppose I can make a point of avoiding the store aisles that are stocked with the C word, but it won't help. It will find me. I'm a chocolate magnet.

"I can still drink coffee?" I inquired, silently calculating the balance on my Starbuck's card.

"Sure."

Six pairs of eyes stared at me as I let out a sigh of relief big enough to fill a hot air balloon.

Technically, mocha isn't chocolate, is it?

CHAPTER TEN

It's Better to Feel Good Than to Spin Good

~ Squashing the Flu Bug ~

While few can argue that modern day plate spinners have near superhuman multitasking capabilities, I recently discovered that none of us are impervious to the microcosm commonly referred to as the "flu bug."

I knew it had infiltrated my home when our youngest crawled between my husband and I at two in the morning, mumbling something about "gonna be sick." Not hearing the "I think I'm" that preceded this, we were utterly unprepared for the sensory onslaught that followed—the dreadful sound of him retching, the not pleasant aroma of said retch, and the unfortunate feel of it underfoot as we followed him into the bathroom.

As I tended to our now-sobbing child, cleaning him off and changing him into clean jammies, my husband pulled the linens off of our bed and began the first of many loads of laundry. Declaring the room uninhabitable, he took to the couch as I squeezed into bed next to my ailing child, thanking my lucky stars that it was the weekend and I could maybe sleep in a few extra minutes.

Despite copious hand washing and consumption of over-the-counter flu prevention products, the bug infiltrated me like so many ants at a summer picnic. Yet, while it knocked me off my feet, I rested easy knowing that my plates were still being spun, or so my family assured me.

Should the plate spinner in your family become incapacitated by this virus, rendering even their best laid plans useless, here is a survival guide to see you through.

First and foremost, before the first sniffle has you rifling through your pockets for a crumpled Kleenex, know who you can call for back up—the neighbor who takes her kids to the same school you do, the grocery store that offers home delivery, and the take-out place that can deliver something vaguely resembling a square meal.

Next, before that first wave of nausea has you checking the headlines to see if anything you've eaten in the past twenty-four hours is being recalled by the FDA, become well-versed in your company's sick leave policy. Most require you to call your immediate supervisor by the time you normally begin your workday. If you wait until he or she is busy calling the authorities to determine the cause of your otherwise unexplained absence, your motives for sparing your peers from the same fate will likely fall on deaf ears.

Finally, in the event that you find yourself lying in your bed with a cold washcloth pressed to your forehead and a thermometer dangling precariously from the side of your mouth, know that your children, future plate-spinning aficionados, can take over on your behalf. If you hear pots and pans clanging in the kitchen, know that they're preparing their own well-balanced meals. If the sound of laughter emanates from their rooms, feel confident that they're beside themselves with delight over their homework assignments.

And, if you notice the night-light in your room flicker off, don't worry. It's either a faulty light bulb or a blown fuse. And really, what are the chances that your kids tried running the washing machine, a videogame system, and the microwave all from the same outlet?

Come to think of it, maybe the better idea is to just get the shot...

~ Flu Me Once ~

Temperatures are dropping, winds are blowing, leaves are falling, and noses are beginning to drip. With another seasonal shift upon us, threats to plate spinners' meticulously choreographed schedules are just an uncontained sneeze away.

Nothing tests a plate-spinner's mettle more than having a sick child. Despite school districts' valiant attempts to disinfect, at this time of year, classrooms transform into full-scale petri dishes. While precaution is key, even if you hose your child down with hand sanitizer, they still risk catching something that will cause their temperature to creep upward, thus prompting a call to you, busy at work, from the school nurse or daycare provider, ordering an immediate pickup.

Before my husband took the plunge and became a stay-at-home dad, these phone calls triggered intense negotiations between us as we bartered our rapidly dwindling vacation time against our managers' level of tolerance for another request to leave early so we could pick up a sick child with whom we'd have to stay until they were fever-free for twenty-four hours. After exhausting favors with family and friends, a typical phone-based arm wrestling match—uh, conversation would go as follows:

Her: "Hi, hon. Daycare called."
Him: "In a meeting."
Her: "At your desk?"
Him: "It's your turn."
Her: "Can't. Big deadline."
Him: "Reporting. Quarterly results."
Her: "Boss. Not happy."
Him: "Call coming through."
Her: (Fingernails tapping on desk.)
Him: "Daycare. Both boys sick."

Her: "Better hurry."
Him: "Right! Wait..."
Her: "Bye." (Click.)

When our boys were older, they quickly learned that staying home from school did not necessarily translate into a day spent in front of a video game console. One of our boys actually tried feigning the flu while in sixth grade. After sticking the thermometer in his mouth, my husband left the room to tend to the others.

When he returned, he spied the allegedly sick child holding the thermometer against a hot light bulb. Faced with a day spent in bed where he would remain for the duration, resting and drinking plenty of fluids, he made it to the bus stop in record time.

I have heard stories of calculating parents who, on hearing of a viral outbreak at their child's school, actually gauge the incubation period of the illness, match it up with their calendar and arrange play dates to expose their children to the virus, thereby minimizing any disruption to their schedules. Convenient, perhaps, but some consider this type of malady manipulation extreme. While some inoculations are mandated, the decision to get a flu shot is still a personal decision.

While some contend that they have never received the shot and have never gotten the flu, others assert that after getting the shot, they got the flu. Me? I have never been a fan of having my skin punctured by a pointy, sharp object, but the memory of missing Christmas morning at my Grandma's house when I was seven years old because I was covered with itchy chicken pox still smarts more.

~ Circle of Life ~

The late arrival of the flu season this year brought with it a reminder that life has a funny way of coming full circle—even while we're still spinning in the midst of it. When the virus infiltrated a member of my family, I made a doctor's appointment. Once there, I had to fill in some forms, describe symptoms to the doctor, get the prescriptions, listen to the nurse rattle off instructions, and ask about things to watch for.

Oh, and by the way, the patient was not one of my boys or even my husband. It was my mom.

My plate spinning has taken on a whole new generation.

A bad cough had laid her flat for a week. When she asked me to get a second bottle of over-the-counter cough medicine, specifically requesting "the big one," I paused. What she needed was to be seen by a doctor.

Considering my workload and the fact that it's tax season and I'm in single-parent mode, the thought crossed my mind to ask one of my siblings to take her. But I knew it was my turn.

Snagging a time slot that could be parlayed into an early lunch break, I picked her up with just moments to spare. After getting her situated in the front seat of my car, she nudged her walker toward me, suggesting that it might fit in the trunk.

I waved her off. With the sleek moves of a suburban mom who's collapsed her fair share of strollers, double buggies, and portable playpens, I had that walker flattened and tucked into the backseat in seconds flat.

On the way to the clinic, she assured me that she was feeling much better. I waited until her coughing fit passed before changing the subject, reminiscing about the time when I was so embarrassed that she took me to the doctor's in my flannel nightgown and slippers.

That she brought me there in my pajamas should've tipped me off to the fact that she thought I was pretty sick. Instead, that she came home from work to take me convinced me that I must be on death's door. Worried, I snuggled next to her and made her promise that if I had to get a shot, she'd get me a lollipop.

Turns out, I did get a shot and she made good on her promise.

I also recalled the times she'd take my siblings to the doctor. On their return, the rest of us would inevitably find the crumpled remains of a bag from Burney Bros. Bakery on the table. I could only assume it was part and parcel of a behavior-based bribe.

And so it goes that after the doctor examined her, I escorted Mom down the hall to the lab for some blood work. After reminding me that she hates needles, I promised her that if she was brave I'd get her Chinese food.

She was and I did.

CHAPTER ELEVEN

Spinning Stress-less

~ Don't Leave Home Without It ~

When I'm busy at work, the last thing I want to see pop up on my caller ID is the number of one of my kids' schools. It invariably means one of two things—either I have to pick up a child who is sick or, worse, one of my perfectly healthy children has forgotten something and they need me to bring it to them.
Right. Now.
Because my mother smirks each time I complain to her about my boys' absentmindedness, I suspect that these phone calls must be the result of a curse that she no doubt laid on me each time I tearfully called her from the principle's office because I had forgotten to bring my regular shoes to school. There I'd be, slogging around in my white, buckled-up galoshes that, by the way, clashed horribly with my green plaid parochial school jumper, until she arrived with my Mary Janes or, years later, platform shoes.
Yes, I was a repeat offender.
Before we were blessed with children, each time I headed out the door on my way to work, my husband (aka, "The Enabler"), would run me through our official household departure checklist: Keys? Check. Purse? Check. Lunch? Check. It's not that I was an especially forgetful

person. As a novice plate spinner, I just had a lot on my mind.

Then we had kids.

After enrolling our first child in daycare, we quickly adapted our checklist to include the ever-vital diaper bag and said baby. Piece of cake. Adding another baby shortly thereafter did little to alter the efficiency with which we left our house as we each balanced a baby, a briefcase, and a diaper bag. Welcoming our third son, however, we bid adieu to efficiency. At that point, I was happy to make it out the door wearing shoes that were the same color, let alone a matched pair.

When our boys started school, we resurrected our checklist. Our high-schoolers head out the door first, still groggy in the dark of the early winter morning. We gently ask so as not to wake them: Homework? Check. Books? Check. Lunch? Check. Gym uniforms? Check. Library books? Check. Off they go. Later in the morning, we repeat the exercise with our younger boys.

On a recent morning, when the boys were gone and the house once again quiet, my husband headed to the kitchen, offering to get me some coffee.

Eager to escape into my home office, I tripped on something in the foyer. Just as I looked down at a rather large running shoe, the phone rang and I heard my husband answer it, asking, "What did you forget?"

As he hung up, I heard him mumble, "The apple doesn't fall far from the tree."

Handing him the shoe, I gasped. "You don't mean me, do you?"

With a wink, he replied, "Check."

~ *Pass the Hat* ~

According to the calendar, it's spring—a turbulent, stress-inducing season. One day it's warm and sunny, the next it's windy and threatening snow. All the while, our calendars are filling up with Easter celebrations, spring sporting events, and graduations.

At this time of year, it's no wonder that even the most self-assured spinner is at risk for the dreadful condition known as over-spinning. Symptoms include feeling very busy, but not especially productive and in complete control, but entirely overwhelmed.

Unfortunately, most plate spinners don't even realize they're afflicted until they are well within its clutches. Remedies, some healthier than others, vary. Harried plate spinners can turn to counseling or meditation, while others simply scrap their responsibilities in exchange for a spot on a remote beach.

When over-spinning threatens to unnerve me, my thoughts turn to imported chocolate. My mother, on the other hand, turned to hats. I came to this conclusion when I was quite young.

After spending a frenzied morning preparing us for a trip to the beach, packing sandwiches, flip-flops, suntan lotion, beach balls, and pails and shovels, my parents braved traffic congested with hundreds of other families who had the same idea. When we finally arrived, I sat digging my toes in the sand and watched as my mom pulled on the most ridiculous-looking swim cap, festooned with a rainbow of floppy bows.

As she tucked her hair up under it, I noticed her posture relax and saw a wide smile spread over her face. I assumed it was the hat and made a mental note to get one for my older sister who was still ranting about me giving her Barbie dolls haircuts.

Before getting down on yourself about not being able to keep aloft as many plates as you'd like, remember that no one wears more hats than a plate spinner. On a typical day, you may find yourself donning any number of virtual chapeaus while you assume the roles of chef, limo driver, banker, or nurse.

My Mom took on these same roles, but kept it together by being a plate-spinning fashionista. Back when women covered their heads with pillbox hats and men wore fedoras, she followed the trends and did her best to make sure that her daughters followed. Dutifully, I tolerated at least one Easter bonnet for the obligatory photo op. Somewhere along the way, though, I turned my back on this fashion accessory.

With the exception of bad hair days, my head remains bare. However, having given up chocolate for Lent, during my most stressful moments, I have found myself prowling the stores for a swim cap.

~ Making the List ~

Sleep. It's something this plate spinner has a love/hate relationship with. I would just as soon end a sentence with a preposition as I would designate eight hours of my day to spend completely unconscious and drooling on my pillow. Yet, the benefits of sleep are well-documented and, I readily concede, so are the affects of sleep deprivation—kryptonite to any high-functioning plate spinner.

Still, sleep and I have a checkered past. It dates back to my early pre-caffeine days. Like it or not, bedtime on school nights was 8:00 pm sharp. I vividly remember laying there, wide awake, listening to the theme music of *Laugh In* coming from the TV in our living room. Not exactly lullaby material. When I'd still be awake to hear Ed McMahon announce, "Here's Johnny!" I knew sleep and I were just not going to get along.

I don't remember being especially hard to rouse, though. That was my older brother's department. On Christmas mornings, when our parents would declare that we couldn't open a single gift until he joined us, my sisters and I always rose to the occasion. Armed with squirt guns and as much patience as we could muster, we'd have him awake and happily tearing through presents in no time flat.

These days, my brother would enjoy the fact that I seem to be suffering from some cruel form of reverse insomnia. Falling asleep is a breeze. It's staying asleep that I'm having problems with. It brings out the worst in me and my grammar. While I've tried all sorts of ways to rectify the matter—everything from deep breathing to watching C-SPAN to reading my AP style manual, I have found that nothing works better than making a list.

The act of transferring the "to dos" swirling around in my head to paper relieves the burden entirely. The list, however, is never-ending. Even at the end of my most productive days, a stray task will wake me up at 3:00 am, nagging at me to get up and write it down. Granted, I may not always be able to make out what I scribble down during the course of the night. It's not unusual for my family to find me, first thing in the morning, squinting at a piece of paper, trying to determine if I am supposed to "buy garbage stickers" or "bag gorilla slickers."

 Choosing to not be hampered by this sleep disruption, I consider it the first tier of my three-level, no-fail wake up system. If, after transferring the item to my list, I happen to fall back to sleep, my alarm clock stands at the ready. In the event of a power outage, there's always the last resort—a child, and I'm not naming names, packing a loaded squirt gun and thinking that waking me up is more important than making it to second grade.

~ *Savoring Summer* ~

With the last day of school several weeks behind us, as a plate spinner with school-aged children, I've been taking advantage of the long, somewhat less-encumbered days of summer by sleeping in just a bit more, lounging at the pool, weather permitting, and, instead of slaving over a hot Crock-Pot all day, cooking on the grill. Having lulled myself into a false sense of relaxation, I was recently jolted to my senses by the appearance of school supplies on store shelves—a blaring reminder that the new school year is just around the corner.

While some plate spinners may have had the opportunity to take advantage of school-sponsored fundraisers offering pre-packaged school supplies that will magically appear on their child's desk prior to the first day of class, others of us may have declined, not wanting to miss out on the thrill of the hunt for erasers, loose-leaf paper, and gallon-sized plastic bags (what these have to do with a child's learning experience, I do not know, but apparently, they're necessary). For this adrenaline-charged group, the members of which who have yet to so much as glance at their children's school supply lists, store ads touting the best prices on these items serve as a battle cry.

In my house, before planning any supply-stocking excursion, I check our lists against what we already have in our bulging school supply bin—a large plastic container into which we deposit items left over from the previous year as well as extra inventory accumulated when we've stockpiled on things not necessarily needed at the start of the school year, but irresistibly priced during the school year. These come in particularly handy if, in the event that one of the boys tells us the night before a big project is due that he needs some construction paper, poster board, or glitter glue, we're covered. As I pry off the lid, I am relieved to see that no one's half-empty lunch bag was dumped, forgotten, along with stubby, eraser-less pencils and cracked plastic rulers.

With five boys at three different levels of their education—one in elementary, two in middle school, and two in high school, I set my plates aloft and review the lists, noting the variance in length between the youngest and oldest. While our kindergartner's is full of items easily pulled from the bin, our high-schoolers' appear to need fewer, but costlier items like a graphing calculator, new running shoes, and a new car. Recognizing my oldest's handwriting, I ignore the last entry.

List in hand, I begin checking off items while rummaging through the bin's contents. Trying in vain to convince my youngest that an old Sponge Bob lunch bag is still cool in a retro sort of way, my middle school boys begin assessing the condition of last year's backpacks.

Next, I confer with my high-schoolers.

My soon-to-be sophomore shrugs. "A couple notebooks and some pens ought to do it."

Check.

Heading for the door, car keys in hand, my oldest hurriedly blurts, "Don't worry about it. I'm good."

A nice pause before the "outfitting-the-dorm-room" shopping we'll be immersed in this time next year. I skeptically watch as he leaves, wondering how much time the rest of us can squeeze in over at the pool before it closes.

~ Sizing Up Summer Break ~

With summer break in sight, my boys are making no effort to hide their excitement over the promise of long, unstructured days. I, on the other hand, am torn. If anything, my workload will intensify, and with kids afoot, I'll have that many more plates to spin. Unlike my older boys who have internships, mission trips, and cross-country practice to fill much of their time, my younger guys are in danger of wiling away their break plopped in front of the Wii. Unstructured, yes, but their summer would hardly be a true break.

Tempted as I am to let them run around with the sprinkler in the backyard and install a deadbolt on my home office door, I may resort to enrolling them in swim lessons at our park district and a camp or two.

Still it saddens me to think that they won't be able to enjoy anything close to the carefree summers I experienced as a kid.

Having spent my summers completely untethered, I am none the worse for wear. My sister and I would leave our house after breakfast and not return until we heard our dad's trademark wolf whistle. No one ever worried where we were, if we remembered to pack a snack, if we forgot our water bottle, or if we remembered to slather ourselves in sunscreen. There wasn't a cell phone or video game in sight.

The smooth streets and sidewalks of our relatively new neighborhood beckoned and we would spend hours on end riding our bikes and roller-skating with our friends. The mark of a good summer was how bleached out our hair got, how tan we were, and how many scars we had on our kneecaps.

It just wouldn't be summer, though, without a trip to the emergency room. The doctors were on a first name basis with my sister, who was a frequent visitor, starting with the time she stepped on a two-by-four that had a nail sticking out of it. Then there was the time she wiped out on her bike at the end of our block. None of us saw exactly what happened, but we heard it. Her bike's screeching tires, the metal crumpling, and a loud *oof* as her body thumped on the cement. By the time we reached her, her tangled Schwinn was in a heap on the grass and she was lying on the sidewalk clutching her knee. We did our best to help her home. Once school started again, dressed in her plaid parochial skirt, she proudly showed off her scars like a badge of honor. Good times.

    Knock on wood, aside from a bad bee sting and a cell phone that was mortally wounded when it took an unscheduled dip in the pool, my boys have enjoyed injury-free summers. Still, not wanting to tempt fate, maybe it would be a good idea to get a well-stocked first aid kit before school lets out. I can leave it out by the sprinkler.

~ Cool Ideas for a Sweltering Summer ~

The last thing a busy plate spinner needs is sweaty hands. Since gloves just aren't a good look for me—especially with shorts and a tank top, I try to avoid the feel of hot, humid air on my skin as much as possible.

To say that summer isn't one of my favorite seasons would be like saying Donald Trump isn't hurting for cash.

Still, when the heat indices climb into triple digits, keeping cool can certainly be a challenge. With every ceiling fan in the house whirring on warp speed, our household cooling system is doing all it can to keep up the outrageous demands I keep putting on our ancient thermostat. I set it to seventy-two—it inches up to seventy-five. I set it to sixty-eight—it brazenly escalates to eighty.

Theoretically, the pool should offer some relief. However, the thought of standing side-by-side with other sweltering bodies in the scorching sun and in water that is warm enough to cook a chicken—well, it just doesn't hold any appeal.

As I write this, I am saving my file every few keystrokes for fear the power company might come knocking.

The thought of no A/C in this balmy weather is one dreadful prospect.

Of course, in the event that ComEd can't keep up with demand, it would be smart to have a backup plan. Yes, there are cooling centers peppered throughout highly-populated areas, but I'd like to suggest the following backup plan just in case you'd like to take matters into your own sweaty hands.

1. Keep the windows and doors closed for as long as possible to keep the artificially-cooled air inside. Restrict any extraneous movement, including any and all housework.

2. Eat the entire inventory of popsicles and ice cream bars in your freezer before they liquefy. Save the sticks to make handheld fans (à la Martha Stewart).
3. Shimmy into your swimwear, even if you wouldn't be caught dead wearing it in public. Remember, you can find a world of forgiveness in a yard of spandex.
4. Ladies, make a quick dash to your garden to snag a flower blossom and tuck behind your ear. Guys, do the same, but be sure to retain the stem, so you can clench it between your teeth.
5. Put little umbrellas in all of the beverages you serve your family—everything from chocolate milk to Hawaiian Punch to bottled water.
6. Pull a Don Ho single out of the box of records you inherited when your parents downsized, pop it onto your kids' Fischer Price turntable and *crank* it.
7. Teach the kids a hula line dance.
8. Host a faux luau by having your young ones rhythmically drum on upturned pots and your older ones wave the grill lighters (set to "high flame") in the air while you serve up PB&Js sprinkled with shredded coconut.
9. After the kids go to bed, set up a couple of lawn chairs next to the filled kiddie pool in the backyard and invite your sweetie to join you for a drink "on the beach."

There...now don't you feel cooler? Aloha oe!

~ A Foreigner to Free Time ~

As this week dawned, my family calendar was awash in white space. No Scouts, no team practices, no work hours for my husband or I. Nothing. A rare trifecta, my kids had spring break, I was able to seize a well-timed pause between projects, and my husband, typically up to his tax tables in returns at this time of year, cautiously admitted that a vacation might be imminent.

This didn't seem possible a few weeks back. Deep in the clutches of my unrelenting schedule, when I could only surface for air between work, chauffeuring the kids, grocery shopping, cleaning, laundry, and all of the other superhero stuff working parents do, I had a fleeting day dream.

I boarded a boat bound for Free Time, a land where all manner of to-do's were banned. Once there, I'd have to declare my intent to relax and rejuvenate before the customs officials would even stamp my passport. Safe within its borders, I would sleep in, fill my days *want-to's*, and sleep soundly at night without a care in the world.

"Just one day," I sighed wistfully as I stared at the image of a project schedule on my laptop monitor, unaware that I had not yet pressed the mute button on my phone.

"One day? Really?" My program manager seemed quite pleased.

Slapped back into reality, I blinked, trying to discern what I had just committed to.

Fumbling, I replied, "Uh, no, wait—let me get back to you on that."

And so here we are, on day three of our visit to Free Time. My husband, skittish about mingling with the locals, has done little more than dip his toe in Lake Free Time, working nearly as much as he did with an appointment-packed schedule.

"Good thing we didn't plan a trip away somewhere, huh?" he sagely announced when he walked through the door last night.

As for me, I reluctantly crossed my fingers while vowing, in the presence of the Free Time customs officers, to relax and rejuvenate. As a result, assimilating to this strange place is impossible. Try as I might, I still wake up at the usual 5:30 am and my lists are still rife with to-do's.

Since I'm here illegally, I've decided to don my June Cleaver disguise, pearls and all. No one, and I mean *no one*, will recognize me as I make waffles, from scratch, and get a jump on the grocery shopping, cleaning, and laundry just so I can see to it that the boys make the most of their time here.

So far, so good. No one's blown my cover, and they have fully immersed themselves in the Free Time culture. Sleeping in until 9:00 am or later, they fill their days with video games, trips to the movies, and basically whatever the heck they want—as long as it doesn't land anyone in the emergency room.

And, while they're away, I try to resist the pull of my work laptop lest I be deported—which would be a shame, really, because I would very much like to return someday. Alone.

CHAPTER TWELVE

Good Plates Don't Bounce

~ Father's Day in Memoriam ~

The third Sunday of June is fast approaching. For most plate spinners, it's time to look for a gift that the paternal figure in their lives will love.

For others, though, it's a day best skipped. Separated from their fathers by distance or death, many children of all ages spend their day in quiet reflection.

I admit—I've rarely given this second group a second thought.

I am always so busy trying to figure out what new thing I can get my husband—the guy who keeps claiming he already has all he ever wanted.

If I just took a clue from my sister, Ann, it might save me the trouble. She always gets her husband of nearly thirty-six years the same thing—an outing to a Kane County Cougars game with the whole family.

Until this year.

Don, my brother-in-law and the other half of my sister since they started dating at sixteen, passed away very recently. He was relatively young and fit. On hearing the news, my thoughts immediately turned to Ann. Then, one by one, I began thinking of my niece and nephews, worrying about how they'd cope. Although grown, their lives had radically changed in an instant.

I pushed back my own fond memories and despair as I clutched my boys and whispered in their ears, "No tears. Uncle Don wouldn't want you crying now."

As we huddled around my sister and her kids like a human cocoon made up of extended family members, we tried our best to cushion the blow. Small gestures like making phone calls, helping with arrangements, bringing food, and doling out hugs, were all we could do to stave off the nagging feeling of helplessness.

The next night, we gathered again at her house to prepare photo displays for his visitation. Some would be on poster boards—some would be on a continually-running DVD that would play at the funeral home while friends, colleagues, and distant relatives arrived to pay their respects.

We popped it in and turned on the TV. With Sinatra singing "My Way," we blinked back the tears and relived the highlights of his life starting with his baptism, moving onto a fishing trip with his dad, group shots with his siblings, a high school prom picture with my sister, and all of the Christmases, birthday parties, weddings, and new babies that came after.

As the tape ended, my sis dabbed her eyes and let out a long sigh before proclaiming, "Well, no Cougars game this year."

As we all hung our heads in reverence, she quietly promised, "Maybe next year."

We turned our attention to the blank poster boards and piles of old pictures. It was time to assemble the tapestry of Don's life.

Each image told a story about the man, always ready with a smile and a joke, who loved his family above all else and would do anything for anyone, no questions asked. It was a fitting tribute to a beloved husband, grandfather, brother, uncle, and son, but for the most part, a dad who had all he ever wanted.

~ *9/11 and the Spoils of Change* ~

For my post-JFK generation, 9/11 is that one pivotal event that has the capacity to spring forth from our memories with all of the raw emotion that the actual day held simply at the mention of it. Even this many years on.
Despite the time that has passed, I can still vividly recall exactly where I was and what I was doing—maybe not when the first plane hit the first tower at the World Trade Center, but when my heart sank into my stomach with a sickening thud as I heard that a second jet, full of innocent people, had just sliced into the second tower like a knife through butter.
Life as we knew it had just changed forever. We couldn't begin to fathom how much, but I knew there was no going back.
There I was, a by-the-book, career-before-family, executive wannabe, and the first thing I did was stand up at my desk, phone to my ear, doing a headcount of my team, much like a mother checking on her brood when she's out in public. While some started whispering, sharing snippets they had heard from family and friends watching the news at home or from our painfully slow Internet access, others began filling my office—usually not a voluntary action.
Project meetings, client presentations, and corporate earnings were the farthest things from all our minds. The small, anxious crowd that was gathering around my desk, hoping to duck out early to be with loved ones, all but shouted, "We are under attack."
As I heard myself telling, not asking, my VP that I would be releasing my team early that day, I felt the change kick in. Like it or not, I was morphing into a protective, maternal human. I just wasn't sure I was ready to admit it.
For the first time in a long time, my instinct was to be with my family. After that, all I really wanted to do was

wrap myself in a flag and go pound the snot out of the bullies who invaded our great playground and played ever so badly with the other kids.

    The next day, flaunting a pair of uncharacteristically big and unabashedly patriotic American flag earrings, I hammered out an email to the CEO, demanding to know why the real ones flying in front of our building were not at half-mast. Later that morning, the poor guy had the misfortune of blocking my access to the coffee machine in the cafeteria. But the day was far from over.

    At my sons' soccer practice that evening, the other mothers were there. Not a briefcase or pair of pantyhose in sight.

    I usually kept my distance, always from the outside looking in. They weren't, after all, plate spinners like me. They didn't drive off to a job every day or hold tight to aspirations of corporate grandeur like I did.

    But that night, under the plane-less and eerily quiet sky, we were all the same. Just a bunch of moms. We chatted a bit, then huddled close as if we all knew—there was no going back. And I, for one, was glad.

ABOUT THE AUTHOR

Barbara is an award-winning novelist and second-generation journalist. After spending a decade in maternity clothes, she has five boys to show for it and much fodder for her column, The Plate Spinner Chronicles, a long-running feature in the *Chicago Tribune*. A member of RWA's Windy City chapter, she still dreams of the day when her to-do list includes "Send NY Times book critic thank you note" and "Accept Godiva's request to be a taste-tester."

To learn more about Barbara, visit her online at www.barbaravalentin.com

Enjoyed this book? Check out the romantic comedy novels in the *Assignment: Romance* series, featuring the fictional "Plate Spinner!" Now in print and all ebook formats from Gemma Halliday Publishing:

Mattie Ross is the *Chicago Gazette's* advice columnist, The Plate Spinner. But her latest assignment—training for the Chicago Marathon—has her paired up with the last man she'd ever want to train with...or fall for!

False Start
available now!

Claire is a burned out breadwinner ready to ditch her quest for happily-ever-after, and her husband, Paul, has traded his high-powered job for life as a stay-at-home dad. But when Claire drafts a letter to the Plate Spinner, both of their lives change forever...

Help Wanted
available now!

www.GemmaHallidayPublishing.com

Made in the USA
Columbia, SC
17 April 2017